A MESS OF IGUANAS,
A WHOOP OF GORILLAS

A MESS
A WHOOP

OF IGUANAS, OF GORILLAS

AN AMAZEMENT OF ANIMAL FACTS

By Alon Shulman

Illustrated by Andy Watt

PARTICULAR
BOOKS

An Imprint of Penguin Books

PARTICULAR BOOKS

Published by the Penguin Group
Penguin Books Ltd, 80 Strand, London WC2R 0RL, England
Penguin Group (USA) Inc., 375 Hudson Street, New York, New York 10014, USA
Penguin Group (Canada), 90 Eglinton Avenue East, Suite 700, Toronto, Ontario, Canada M4P 2Y3
(a division of Pearson Penguin Canada Inc.)
Penguin Ireland, 25 St Stephen's Green, Dublin 2, Ireland
(a division of Penguin Books Ltd)
Penguin Group (Australia), 250 Camberwell Road, Camberwell, Victoria 3124, Australia
(a division of Pearson Australia Group Pty Ltd)
Penguin Books India Pvt Ltd, 11 Community Centre, Panchsheel Park, New Delhi – 110 017, India
Penguin Group (NZ), 67 Apollo Drive, Rosedale, North Shore 0632, New Zealand
(a division of Pearson New Zealand Ltd)
Penguin Books (South Africa) (Pty) Ltd, 24 Sturdee Avenue,
Rosebank, Johannesburg 2196, South Africa

Penguin Books Ltd, Registered Offices: 80 Strand, London WC2R 0RL, England

www.penguin.com

First published 2009
1

Copyright © Alon Shulman, 2009

Illustrations copyright © Andy Watt 2009

ISBN: 978–1–846–14255–0

This book is dedicated to my parents, Emma and Neville Shulman, whose inspiration, support and love are always with me.

To both these wonderful people who gave me life I am eternally grateful.

CONTENTS

ACKNOWLEDGEMENTS

This book has been a joy to write and that is largely due to the invaluable contribution of several people who I would like to acknowledge:

My editor, Helen Conford, for her incredible enthusiasm and support throughout this project and Mari, Alex, Gina and the team at Penguin;

My good friend and agent, Sophie Hicks, and everyone at Ed Victor Ltd;

Andy Watt, for providing me with so many wonderful illustrations;

Lauren, Lee & Isa & Rose, Catherine Morse, Steve Hayes, Jimmy Choo, Kettan Vara, Ken and Susannah Bates, Jane Goodall, Ishi Ben David, Ridley Scott, Peter Jäderberg, Robert Barbieri, Peter Chow, James Saville, Jackie Robins and Laurie Milne for showing interest;

My late grandparents Anne, Batia, Felix and Jack for getting the ball rolling.

A huge thank you to all of you – Alon Shulman

Andy Watt would like to thank his mum and dad, Nick, Charlotte, Josie and Caz at Folio, Jim Stoddart and Helen Conford at Penguin, Alon for letting me draw it my way, Gerald Scarfe for his words of encouragement, Maurice and Shona at Warwickshire College School of Art, the late great Tony Hart, and the legend that is Rolf Harris … cheers!

INTRODUCTION
ON THE ORIGINS OF COLLECTIVE NOUNS

I was heading towards Angel Falls in Venezuela through the rainforest with my local guide whose name was Legarta Negra. He was barefoot and stopped every few paces to point out the local fauna and flora or to chew on an ant or two (more to shock me I think than for a filling snack). We had seen iguanas, spiders, incredible birds and insects aplenty as we picked our way across the tree roots on our journey to the tallest waterfall in the world. For many, Angel Falls is the most dramatic of waterfalls, spilling into a free fall for almost one kilometre before crashing into the pool below. I asked him what his name meant and he replied, 'Black Lizard, you know, like the herd of iguanas.' My immediate thought was that a group of iguanas is known as 'a mess of iguanas' and I spent the rest of the day thinking about all the collective nouns of the animals I had seen on the trip ranging from insects to birds. On the way back to the UK I bought a beautiful carved wooden iguana which I have looked at every day since and which finally motivated me to put together the terms for groups of animals with some interesting facts about them.

There are many wonderful creatures on the Earth and there are many words in every language that relate to animals from their size and appearance to their sounds and way of life. Phrases attributed to human activity based on animal behaviour are numerous. We all know of someone who is as busy as a beaver, as wise as an owl, drinks like a fish, works like a dog, eats like a pig or is as quiet as a mouse. It is estimated that there are currently 1.4 million animal species known to science at this time and possibly as many as 30 million species on the planet. Amazingly more than 90 per cent of all the animal species that have ever lived on Earth were extinct before the coming of man. Each unique species has contributed to our rich language as well as to the environment it lives in. Many of the creatures we know today have evolved in unrecognizable ways: reptiles were responsible for such body-part innovations as feathers, claws, furs, differentiated teeth, water-impervious skin, water-impervious eggs and the penis. Animals have had to adapt to be able to compete with and survive alongside other species of animals and in some cases plants. There are currently approximately 600 species of plants that are carnivorous. Carnivorous plants mostly eat insects although some eat frogs, birds and even small monkeys. There is an incredible diversity of living creatures and a seemingly infinite amount of information about them, from their Latin names and classification to their evolution and behaviour. And yet it is still the collective nouns for the individual animals that remain the most sought-after information. The collective nouns interest and amuse everyone from academics to pub quizzers, inquisitive kids, language buffs, internet bloggers and wannabe know-it-alls.

I was always fascinated with interesting facts. As a child I loved trivia and would delight my parents' friends by telling them for no apparent reason that 85 per cent of all life on Earth is plankton or that no new animals have been domesticated in the past 4,000 years. My favourite was always that the oceans contain 99 per cent of the living space on the planet which I always thought opened up amazing possibilities for the future. One day I came across the phrase 'gaggle of geese' in some school homework and I was surprised – I had thought this was a made-up phrase used to entertain small children. Never having seen wild geese or heard them 'gaggle' as a child I'd just assumed that they 'quacked'. I looked up this collective noun in the *Oxford English Dictionary*, found it to be correct ... and so began to collect the collective nouns for animals. I was also interested in the sounds that animals made. Not just from the thrilling onomatopoeic sense, but I was curious if these sounds had correct names. I could just about grasp the difference between a roar and a growl but I wondered if there was a word to describe the unique sounds an individual creature made. I remember reading that the sound of the shearwater is called a 'shrill' and that started another strand of fact collecting. I have included the correct terms for some of these sounds among the facts in this book.

Despite many of the collective nouns for animals being regarded as unusual, people often use very descriptive nouns as the conventional terms for groups of animals and birds – 'a parliament of rooks', 'a murder of crows'. The most widely known collective term (other than the good old 'gaggle of geese') is a 'pride of lions'. This is now so embedded as a term that people often don't remember the most common definition of pride when they say it. Interestingly, birds seem to have the widest range of unusual terms to describe them, such as 'a wobble of ostriches'. It is often assumed that the terms are recent inventions but in fact the origins of many modern-sounding collective nouns, including 'a pride of lions', have their written origins in documents and poetry dating back as far as the fifteenth century. It is interesting that as language has evolved most of the original collective terms have remained with us.

Recording animals' unusual or colourful collective terms is believed to have originated from early English hunting traditions and a rarely used synonym for collective nouns for animals is 'terms of venery' with venery relating to the act of hunting. It is interesting that as language has evolved most of the so-called terms of venery have remained unchanged although some more archaic terms have been replaced or simply faded away, such as 'a haras of horses' which does not seem to have been used much since the fifteenth century and is often incorrectly replaced with the generic 'herd'. There are many fanciful collective nouns bandied about such as 'a stench of schnauzers' and 'a dissimulation of birds', but I have tried to stick to linguistically correct and commonly used collective nouns.

Collective nouns for animals were originally made up by gentlemen out on a hunt, fusing their passion for hunting with an interest in language. Hunting, or venery as it was known up until the seventeenth century, was considered an important pastime which helped the aristocracy in times of peace practise skills they would need to use in battle. Rules regarding hunting practices were introduced to Britain by William the Conqueror and the traditional cry of 'tally-ho' is derived from the Norman French 'il est haut' literally meaning 'he [the stag] is up [and running]'. These regulations were not only to govern how to hunt but what to hunt. By 1340 the four beasts of the hunt, or of venery, were the hare, the hart, the wolf and the wild boar and the five beasts of the chase were the buck, the doe, the fox, the marten and the roe. The aristocracy started putting land aside for the purpose of hunting and created laws to protect the animals on the land from poachers. The importance of game and its elitist connotations can be seen in the popular Robin Hood legends, in which one of the main charges against the 'merry men' is that they 'hunt the King's deer'. Creating collective terms for the animals the huntsmen encountered simply consisted of thinking up amusing and often outlandish collective terms for the animals and birds encountered while out hunting. Most of these were used in oral exchange and may have been changed as regularly as on a daily basis at the time without being recorded – a bit like not saving the high score on a computer game today. We can only wonder what incredible collectives didn't make it into the written record and have been lost forever.

As recreation and leisure activities became more desirable to the nobility so hunting, pastimes and games became more widespread. Interestingly in this context, the term 'game' was first used in about 1290 to refer to 'wild animals caught for sport' with the meaning broadening to include a 'contest played according to rules' and it was around this period that words and phrases relating to hunting, wild animals, domestic animals, birds, fish and even mythical animals began to enter both spoken and written language. Collective terms started to appear in texts on hunting and what had begun as a private verbal exchange between very few people became more and more widely available.

Edward II's huntsman, William Twici, penned *Le Art de Vénerie* in 1328 formalizing certain hunting rules. The royal seal of approval reached its peak in about 1389 when Edward, Duke of York, translated the *Livre de la Chasse* (Book of the Hunt) by Gaston Phoebus into English. Styling himself as the author, Edward's translation (entitled *The Master of Game*) is the oldest English book on hunting. To be fair to Edward it wasn't total plagiarism as he added five chapters regarding the practice of hunting and of game management in England. His opening dedication was originally to his brother Henry, Prince of Wales (the future Henry V) but was erased and replaced with 'Here begynnethe a boke that his clepid Master of the Game was made and compilid be my Lorde of yorke to be called cheftayne of alle maner of disporte of huntyng and of venery. The boke made and compilid togedir be the information of Sir Thomas of kerderston Knyghte ye that lyketh to loke over this booke may fynde fulle notable tretys and sovereyne of that longethe to al maner of huntynge.' Interestingly, for such an influential work *The Master of The Game* was long copied and circulated but was not actually printed until 1904.

It is in the fourteenth and early fifteenth centuries that words and phrases to describe animals start to appear on a reasonably regular basis. The term 'rabble' was first used in about 1300 to refer to a 'pack of animals' and was only first used to mean 'a tumultuous crowd of people' in 1513. 'School' is first used in about 1400 with reference to a group of fish and although this has stuck it arrived in the language in error when 'schole' meaning 'a group of fish or other animals' was misreported (although this is also the origin of 'shoal'). Some collectives even had double meanings such as 'a bevy of quails' which is first recorded in around 1430 and was also used when talking about a group of ladies. It is believed that the collective term arrived with reference to birds gathered at a pool for a drink (beverage) and even today 'bevy' is also used for an alcoholic drink as well as for the collective noun for beauties. It is also still common for women to be referred to by men as 'birds'.

The latter half of the fifteenth century is regarded as the golden age of collective nouns. The first important work appeared in about 1450 and is known as *The Egerton Manuscript* and contained 106 terms. This work laid the foundations for recorded collective nouns with terms like a 'mursher of crowys', 'an unkindness of ravens', 'a spring of teal', 'a lepe of lebardis [leap of leopards]' and a 'gagelynge [gaggle] of geese'. This was followed by William Caxton's *The Hors, Shepe & Ghoos* in 1476 which also had 106 terms but included new additions such as 'a flock of lice' and 'a discecion [descent] of woodpeckers' and in which the 'mursher' had evolved into the recognizable 'murther of crowes'. While both these works are key references for modern collective term collectors it is *The Boke of St Albans* by Dame Juliana Barnes from 1486 that is the cornerstone for the widespread interest in the collective nouns of living creatures. Reprinted many times, its 164 collective nouns have on the whole stood the test of time and while some terms have fallen by the wayside it can be argued that this work more than any other before or since established the validity of creating new words (or altering existing ones) as a bona fide contribution to language. This is even visible in the publisher and wordsmith Wynkyn de Worde who adapted his real name, Jan Van Wynkyn, to include reference to his profession. *The Boke of St Albans* gave us many terms which are still in use today. 'A herd of curlews', 'a pride of lions', 'a clowder of cats', 'a sord of mallards', 'a cete of badgers', 'a building of rooks', 'a skulk of foxes', 'a congregation of plovers', 'a dule of doves', 'a shrewdness of apes' and 'a muster of peacocks' are among the many wonderful additions to the language that this book contributes and are still relevant over 520 years later. Not only were new terms added but terms from other sources were updated so 'a labyr of mollys' in Egerton becomes 'a labour of mollis' in St Albans and has now evolved into 'a labour of moles'. Quite clearly a lot of time was spent thinking of these terms while out on a hunt!

Collective nouns also emerged from the most unlikely of sources. This medieval distraction also entered the battlefield when the battle of Rouvrai in 1492 became known as The Battle of the Herrings as it was fought in defence of a convoy of provisions which consisted mostly of herrings and other 'lenten stuffe'. 'An army of herrings' was born. More and more words that we use and recognize today were formed around this time. In 1555 'troglodyte' entered the language to mean 'cave dweller' or more literally 'one who creeps into a hole [trogle]' which has given us 'a trogle of snakes'.

Now that the aristocracy had these wonderful collective terms, they inexplicably switched their focus to hunting game rather than playing games. In 1530, when Hampton Court was taken possession of by Henry VIII he was able to indulge in his passion for hunting, hawking and outdoor pursuits there. He proceeded to acquire all the manors adjacent to Hampton Court and by an Act of Parliament of 1539 united them into a seigneury of several manors held under one baron or lord paramount (known as an 'honour') whereby it was decreed that 'the King shall have therein a chase and free chase and warren, for all beasts of venery and fowls of warren which shall be called Hampton Court Chase'. More and more rules were formulated and most aristocrats would have had a printed version of these, most famously *The Gentleman's Academic* by Gervase Markham which was published in 1595. Subsequent monarchs and governments passed numerous laws and decrees promoting venery and custodians of the King's game. In October 1603 James I appointed the Keeper of Banbury Castle to 'preserve the game of venery and falconry, and to punish all offenders who transgress the laws by shooting, taking of partridges...' and in 1619 James issued a writ under the privy seal to a Henry Jerningham Esq., 'one of the gentlemen of our privie Chamber' which charged him with safeguarding the royal 'game as well of venery as of falconry' in the county of Norfolk. His son Charles I loved hunting deer; this physical sport was Charles's favourite despite having many health issues as a child and only growing to 5ft 3in as an adult. In 1625 Charles brought his court to Richmond Palace to escape the plague in London and in 1637 he enclosed the park for red and fallow deer and regularly feasted on venison which was considered superior to beef. The term 'venison' originally meant the meat of any large game but by Charles's time it was only used in the way we know it today. During these centuries people still created names for groups of animals and collective nouns for these creatures continued to enter our language.

One problem faced by the noble classes as well as the common man was that with so much land being administered for the king it was becoming harder to find places to hunt. It was at this time that fishing started to become an acceptable alternative pastime which brought us new species to be categorized. Izaak Walton's *The Compleat Angler; or, the Contemplative Man's Recreation* published in 1653 became essential reading giving us enduring collective nouns such as 'a quantity of smelts' as they were recorded in 'vast quantities'. It is still in print today and apart from the Bible and *The Book of Common Prayer* no book has been more reprinted.

Collective nouns were being recorded for more and more species and from many new sources, which meant that the origins of these phrases could have many different potential sources. The origin of the term 'a parcel of penguins' is a much disputed collective. The term 'parcel' has been used since about 1645 to refer to a package. Prior to this it was commonly used from 1584 onwards as a verb meaning 'to divide into small portions'. Neither of these have anything to do with penguins. From approximately 1303 onwards 'parcel', originating from the Old French word 'parcelle', was used to describe a 'small piece' or 'part'. This definition is still with us today in the form of a 'parcel of land' and is commonly believed to be where the collective noun for the penguin originated as the sailors would spot land first by the contrast between the snow and the body of the penguins (who could number 50,000 plus). A parcel was also used to describe a group of people or company of soldiers; Shakespeare wrote of 'this youthful parcel of noble bachelors' and an equally strong argument for the origin of 'a parcel of penguins' is the similarity between a group of penguins seeming to stand to attention and a parcel of troops. The true origin comes from the informal American term for a large group which was first recorded in 1835 as a 'passel'. American sailors would refer to 'a passel of penguins' which has passed into record as a parcel of penguins'.

The eighteenth and nineteenth centuries witnessed huge leaps in the discovery of species and of course the publication of Charles Darwin's *Origin of Species* in 1859.

Despite this, the pace of collective noun creation had slowed considerably. William Carr's *The Dialect of Craven ... A Copious Glossary* of 1828 decided that marching caterpillars were 'an army' while Osbaliston's *British Sportsmen* of 1785 gave us 'a wisp of snipe'. Existing terms such as 'flock' and 'herd' began to be thrown at new species. Even new slang phrases such as 'pod' (which was used by American sailors from 1827 to describe whales or seals) quickly appeared attached in certain instances to dolphins, porpoises and even birds. Collective noun creation had become the domain of the largely uneducated sailor. It looked like an ancient art form had been lost.

Luckily, the twentieth century with its huge scientific leaps also sowed the seeds for an expansion in language, both from historical records and from new sources. The collective term 'a grist of bees' was first recorded in the 1930s and 'a convocation of eagles' first appeared in the *Illustrated Sporting and Dramatic News* in 1925.

Of course, there are collective nouns for many things other than animals, but it is the collective nouns for animals that always generate the most interest. At the beginning of the twenty-first century we stand on the shoulders of the three key sources that championed group terms in the twentieth century. The first two were written before the Second World War, in a time when the world was being opened up by air travel but was disrupted by huge conflict that pushed an interest in non-essential language out of prominence. They are the very hard to find *Proper Terms* written by John Hodgkin in 1909 and the excellent *The Language of Sport* written by C. E. Hare in 1939 which was reprinted as *The Language of Field Sports* in 1948 and gives us such modern classics as 'a hover of trout'. Both works add a new and exciting dimension to the accumulation of collective nouns of living creatures. These gems were waiting to be rediscovered and they were by James Lipton (now also world renowned for his TV show *Inside The Actors Studio*). In 1968 Lipton wrote *An Exaltation of Larks* which breathed new life into venery, as applied to the pastime of creating collective nouns. Lipton blended 'group terms, real and fanciful' using nearly all known sources containing lists of beasts of venery. Lipton made a detailed study in his attempt to restore 'the magic to the mundane' and invited his readers to participate in what he termed 'The Game of Venery'. Most of Lipton's recorded terms are invented or at best fanciful but what is exciting about his work is that he has treated the creation of collective terms as a literally (or literary) living and breathing game and so has unwittingly linked this wonderful pastime back to The Royal Game of Ur played over 5,000 years ago in Mesopotamia while paving the way for the medieval pastime of sourcing and creating collective nouns to go forward into the twenty-first century.

Appealing to novices and seasoned veterans alike, the rules of this pursuit are very loose. In the 500-plus years that this 'sport' has been played, no one has actually worked out a way to define winning and losing. Etymologists examine when and how words entered a language and how their meaning and use have changed. Etymological theory recognizes that collective nouns originate through two basic word and phrase creation techniques: borrowing and adoption from other languages; and a physical description of the creature in question including its behaviour and onomatopoeic elements. As many of our modern-day collective nouns originate from a spoken source, some of the alternative terms for a particular group of animals can be clearly traced to the evolution of pronunciation in different areas, hence we have a 'parcel' and a 'passel' of hogs. Regional terms eventually are amalgamated to give the definitive collective noun, while some medieval terms are so specific to the culture of the time that they disappear, such as the now 'extinct' 'blessing of unicorns'.

Often pronunciation and an oral rather than written use of a phrase can lead to a change in the phrase which then becomes fixed in language – often with no record of its origin. The phrase 'donkey's years', which today refers to a long period of time, relates to the long ears of a donkey and is actually first recorded as 'donkey's ears'. The phrase was first recorded in 1916 as donkey's ears and within ten years had changed forever into the modern form. The idea was supported by the belief that donkeys did in fact live a very long time.

On the opposite end of the linguistic spectrum some recently discovered animals have yet to be officially welcomed with a collective term. The okapi, an African animal so secretive it was once believed to be a mythical unicorn, was described in the 1890s by the explorer Henry Morton Stanley as a kind of forest donkey. Okapi, which have a black, prehensile giraffe-like tongue and zebra-like stripes on their behind, were unknown to the Western world until the early twentieth century when the British governor of Uganda, Sir Harry Johnston, sent a complete skin and a skull belonging to the creature to the UK. When an okapi was finally studied in 1901, biologists were astonished to find that its closest living relative was the giraffe. It is worth noting that the first living okapi wasn't photographed in the wild until 2006. This momentous snapshot taken in the Democratic Republic of the Congo proves that the species is still surviving there despite the constant political unrest and civil conflict. At the moment they are known as a herd as despite their huge size they don't tower like their giraffe cousins and the local population has no group term as these wonderful animals are rarely seen.

One species I have deliberately left out of this book on collective nouns is the human being. Human classification is a complex process, ever changing as more groups are created that different humans join or are linked to. *Homo sapiens* is the species to which all living humans belong and is self-named from the Latin where it means 'wise man'. Early forms of *Homo sapiens* coexisted in some parts of the world with other hominid species such as the Neanderthals, who eventually died out, leaving our human ancestors as the most intelligent and some would say successful species on the planet. By about 11,000 BC modern humans had populated almost the entire globe and as of 2008, humans are listed as the species of least concern for extinction by the (human-run) International Union for Conservation of Nature. Unlike any other species it is impossible to give humans one collective noun. As a part of humanity, a word which describes the entire species as well as one of our greatest qualities, we can all be tagged with various labels depending on the size of the group, its behaviour, its location or even its origins. The complexity we exhibit as a species and our genetically programmed instinct to learn has resulted in there being no fixed form of group size as well as no apparent limit to the physical and mental activity that humans are able or willing to carry out. An individual can be a part of many different collective groups at the same time and these groups can range in size enormously, from a family to a nation. Depending on circumstance we can be referred to in many ways including a brigade, a gaggle, a bunch, a team, a cabal, a troupe, a clan, an army, a caste, a community, a tribe, a colony, a society, a cast, a clique, a den, a cohort, a column, a shower, a rabble, a company, a complement, a squad, a contingent, a corps, a panel, a crew, a crowd, a gang, a platoon, a civilization, a posse, a club, a regiment, a cavalcade, a bevy, a congregation, or a unit. We can be categorized by location, religion, belief, nationality, origins and ancestry or even be part of a dynasty consisting of deceased members as well as the living. Stand-alone groups exist within groups and we can even be referred to by characteristics such as a common language, culture or ethnicity which can mean that we are part of a group to which we are only connected by a psychological bond. All this being said and despite giving ourselves labels or being labelled we are part of the human race, which means that despite our differences the largest collective group of humans includes all of us. Uniquely we do not need to be a group or even a herd, flock, pack or colony for no matter what subgroups we are a part of our species is best summed up with the all-encompassing collective term 'humankind'.

From my own research what is apparent is that when it comes to the collective nouns for animals there are no rules. During the course of my research I came across a stare, a wisdom and a study as collective nouns for owls; the correct term is in fact 'a parliament of owls'. Even the highly respected online version of the *Oxford English Dictionary*, considered by many academics to hold the definitive list of correct word usage, often has several collective nouns for the same animal. Some phrases are logical, some make good sense if the animals' habitat is known, such as 'a bed of clams', some if the appearance of the animal is known, such as 'a pride of lions' because of the lion's regal bearing and extravagant mane, some phrases relate to the animals' behaviour such as 'a leap of leopards', others can be understood only if their origins are traced through historical sources, and some relate to the sound an animal makes, such as the trumpeting elephants.

Collective nouns originate in many different ways: through written language, translation, oral tradition and fanciful creation. Written languages developed at a different pace to spoken versions where local circumstances, regional dialects and unique influences shaped the needs of people. Exploration and conquest merged languages as well as introducing new species that needed to be named. As scientific knowledge and understanding of the differences between groups of creatures developed, so more and more terms to describe these animals were needed. Even the word 'animal' changed in its use. First recorded with its current meaning in 1398, 'animal' originated from the Latin 'animalis' which translated as 'living being'. Prior to this the word 'beast' was used, and this remained in common usage until the end of the sixteenth century. The word 'beast' when referring to a wild animal replaced the Old English word 'deor' (deer).

There is often confusion, with people mixing up the collective noun with the habitat, such as the common error with 'a rookery of seals or herons' mentioned in several texts, while some people dispute the 'bed of clams' collective term although in this case the term is correct as the clams do not have a separate habitat to the place that the group is found. Collective nouns are often used to describe a particular type of animal as opposed to a scientifically recorded species or genus; for example, the horseshoe crab, which also is called by the name king crab, is not a crustacean at all, and the hermit crab, although a crustacean, is not a true crab. Even with all these options not all origins are as easy to identify as 'a cackle of hyenas' – some, like 'a smack of jellyfish', just are what they are.

Descriptive words and phrases often change very quickly as populations are subjected to increasingly diverse cultural and linguistic influences. In the First World War the American recruits were known as 'grunts' which is derived from the Old English word 'ground' which became 'groundman' meaning an unskilled railway worker in North America. Doughboys were fried flour dumplings used by Nelson's sailors at Trafalgar and Wellington's troops at Waterloo; the term came to America via the transatlantic migration and was used as a term to describe soldiers as early as 1846. It was the doughboys who arrived in France in 1917. By the Second World War these troops became known as GIs purely because they had 'G.I.', which stood for Government Issue, stamped on all government kit supplies given to recruits. If we continue relating to animals in the way we have over the centuries and in particular the way we have in this age, where understanding the environment and individual ecosystems is so important, it is likely that more and more individual species and subspecies will be re-evaluated and redefined.

As we get to understand more and more about the animals we share the planet with it is likely that more terms to describe groups of animals will emerge. At this point I'd like to mention the plight of poor old 'Lonesome George', a ninety-year-old Pinta Island tortoise whose species was considered extinct until 1971 when he was discovered in the Galapagos. If anyone needs to be part of a group it is George.

As the only known Pinta, he is officially recognized as the rarest animal in the world and unless a female is found or he mates with a female of a neighbouring species whose offspring could then be back-crossed, he will be the end of the line. The more animals that end up like George, the fewer collective nouns we'll have.

So this is a book of collective names for groups of animals and my favourite animal facts, the culmination of my lifetime (so far) fascination with language, facts and with animals. Many will be familiar but others will be unheard of, deriving from medieval witticisms, works of literature and tribal or rural communities. The collective nouns here generally describe any size group of the particular creature. Sometimes an animal will have several different attributed collective nouns depending on its action such as a swan in the air and on water. Birds such as the swan, duck and goose have had their collective terms recorded since the earliest collective listings of medieval times and have been listed alongside game birds and birds used for hunting and hawking. Used by man in many ways including for sport, decoration, food, hunting and as pets, birds naturally contributed greatly to written language.

Normally the action that the animal carries out can be done either alone or as part of a group and does not always refer to its collective noun; for example, it only takes one cow to make up a stampede. Some pairs of animals have their own descriptive term: 'a brace of greyhounds', 'a couple of impala', 'a duet of doves', 'a yoke of oxen' and 'a cast of hawks' when in flight. Some animals even have a name for three of the species such as 'a leash of foxes'. Certain animals shouldn't really have a collective noun, such as ferrets, which are known to be fiercely solitary animals and unlikely to group together. Despite this there are two collective nouns that have been in existence: the commonly used 'business of ferrets' and the now extinct Old Saxon 'fesnying'. Ferrets have featured in all collective noun lists from the earliest on record. White ferrets were the hunters' ferret of choice in the Middle Ages as they were easy to spot in the undergrowth, and Gaston Phoebus' *Book of the Hunt* written in approximately 1389 explains how to use ferrets correctly to hunt rabbits. Extinct and mythical creatures have been omitted, although I have taken the liberty of including 'a pungent of sasquatch', an 'animal' that many believe exists and whose collective name comes from the Native American tribe the Iroquois' word meaning 'foul air'. As well as the strange and humorous there are many terms that have become firmly anchored in everyday use, like 'a string of racehorses', 'a pride of lions' and the good old 'gaggle of geese'. For many people these are run of the mill and unremarkable though as wonderful and unique in origin as any in *The Boke of St Albans*. What is clear is that there is more to groups of creatures than herds, flocks and schools.

The facts I have chosen to accompany the collective noun entries cover a wide cross-section of subjects, ranging from word origin to history, record-breaking and behaviour. These are often unique to the particular species and help to show how the collective noun may have originated. There are many 'facts' in circulation and while some have a grain or two of truth they are in need of verification and so I have decided to leave them out of this book. Some of my favourite examples of these 'facts' are: 'most lipstick contains fish scales'; 'a typical bed usually houses over 6 billion dust mites'; and 'the weight of insects eaten by spiders every year is greater than the total weight of the entire human population'.

All of the collective nouns presented here (and there are 273 of them, compared to 146 in *The Boke of St Albans*) have been verified in one or more dictionaries as well as online referencing. Language constantly evolves and so I'm sure that some terms will be replaced – especially when there are variations on a particular collective noun. Sadly it is inevitable that some of the wonderful creatures in this book will become extinct and so it is records like this that help their memory and contribution to our planet live on – something that Juliana Barnes unwittingly started when she compiled records of collective nouns and secured her place as a footnote in recorded history over 500 years ago.

Alon Shulman
London 2009

LIST OF COLLECTIVE NOUNS

This list comprises the correct phrases to describe groups of animals. I have included nouns used to describe particular groups taking part in various activities such as 'A Kettle' which refers to 'A Committee of Vultures' when they are circling in the air. Within the individual entries in this book I have also additionally listed commonly used collective noun variations as well as correcting some common misconceptions.

An Ambush of Tigers
An Army of Ants
An Army of Caterpillars
An Army of Herrings
An Array of Hedgehogs
An Ascension of Skylarks
An Asylum of Cuckoos
An Asylum of Loons
A Band of Coatimundi
A Band of Nymphs
A Barren of Mules
A Battery of Barracudas
A Bazaar of Falcons

A Bazaar of Guillemots
A Bed of Clams
A Bed of Oysters
A Bevy of Otters
A Bike of Hornets
A Bike of Wasps
A Bind of Salmon
A Bloat of Hippopotami
  (or Hippopotamuses)
A Boogle of Weasels
A Bouquet of Hummingbirds
A Brood of Hens
A Brood of Termites

A Building of Rooks

A Bunch of Ducks
  (*'A Paddling' when on water;*
  'A Flight' when in the air)

A Bunch of Waterfowl
  (*'A Knob' when less than*
  thirty birds; a dense group is
  'A Raft')

A Bunch of Wildfowl

A Bushel of Crabs

A Business of Ferrets

A Cackle of Hyenas

A Cartload of Monkeys

A Cete of Badgers

A Chain of Bobolinks

A Charm of Goldfinches

A Chatter of Budgerigars

A Chattering of Choughs

A Choir of Song Sparrows

A Cloud of Crickets

A Cloud of Flies

A Cloud of Gnats
  (*'A Ghost' for males ready to*
  mate)

A Cloud of Tadpoles

A Clowder of Cats

A Cluster of Antelope

A Cluster of Mussels

A Cluster of Spiders

A Clutch of Eggs

A Coalition of Cheetahs

A Colony of Bats

A Colony of Chinchillas

A Colony of Corals

A Colony of Rats

A Committee of Vultures
  (*'A Kettle' when circling in*
  the air)

A Company of Widgeon

A Confusion of Guinea Fowl

A Congregation of Crocodiles

A Congregation of Eagles

A Congregation of Plovers
  (*'A Wing' in flight*)

A Contradiction of
  Sandpipers

A Covert of Coots
  (*'A Shoal' when swimming*)

A Covey of Grouse

A Covey of Partridges

A Covey of Quails

A Cowardice of Curs

A Crash of Rhinoceroses

A Crowd of Redwing

A Cry of Hounds
  (*three hounds is 'A Couple*
  And A Half')

A Culture of Bacteria

A Dazzle of Zebras

A Deceit of Lapwings

A Descent of Woodpeckers

A Destruction of Wild Cats

A Dopping of Goosander

A Doylt of Swine

A Dray of Squirrels
A Drove of Bullocks
A Drove of Hogs
A Dule of Doves
  (also known as 'A Dole';
  'A Pair' of doves)
An Echo of Mockingbirds
An Exaltation of Larks
A Fall of Woodcocks
A Family of Beavers
A Family of Sardines
A Flamboyance of
  Flamingoes
A Flick of Rabbits
  ('A Herd' when domestic;
  'A Kindle' when young)
A Flight of Albatrosses
A Fling of Dunlin
A Flink of Cows
  (twelve cows)
A Flock of Birds
  ('A Flight' when in the air;
  'A Volary' when in an aviary)
A Flock of Blackbirds
A Flock of Lice
A Flock of Pigeons
  ('A Kit' when in flight)
A Flock of Seagulls
A Flock of Sheep
  ('A Drove' or 'Drift' when
  driven)
A Flock of Swifts

A Flotilla of Frigatebirds
A Gaggle of Geese
A Gam of Porpoises
A Gam of Whales
  (a small gam is 'A Pod')
A Glide of Flying Fish
A Grind of Bottlenose
  Dolphins
A Grist of Bees
A Group of Capybara
A Group of Guinea Pigs
A Group of Humans
A Group of Lemurs
A Grove of American Tree
  Sparrows
A Gulp of Cormorants
A Gulp of Swallows
A Haras of Horses
  ('A Stable' when domesti-
  cated and property)
A Harem of Seals *(a small*
  harem is 'A Pod')
A Hatch of Fleas
A Herd of Asses
  ('A Drove' when driven;
  'A Coffle' when in a roped
  line)
A Herd of Cattle
A Herd of Curlews
A Herd of Oxen
  ('A Team' in harness; a pair is
  'A Yoke')

A Herd of Pigs
A Herd of Wrens
A Hill of Ruffs
A Hoover of Armadillos
A Horde of Gerbils
A Horde of Hamsters
A Horde of Insects
A Host of Sparrows
A Hover of Trout
A Huddle of Walruses
A Husk of Hares
An Implausibility of Gnus
An Implausibility of
  Wildebeest
An Inferno of Lucifer
  Hummingbirds
An Intrusion of Cockroaches
An Invisibleness of
  Ptarmigan
A Kindle of Kittens
A Kine of Cows
A Knob of Toads
A Knot of Frogs
A Labour of Moles
A Lamentation of Swans
  ('A Wedge' in the air;
  'A Bank' on the ground)
A Laziness of Sloths
A Leap of Leopards
A Leap of Lizards
A Leash of Deer
A Leash of Greyhounds

A Litter of Peeps
A Marathon of Roadrunners
A Mess of Iguanas
A Mews of Capons
A Mews of Hawks
  ('A Kettle' when flying; a pair
  is 'A Boil')
A Mob of Emus
A Mob of Meerkats
A Murder of Crows
A Murmuration of Starlings
A Muster of Peacocks
A Mustering of Storks
  ('A Phalanx' when migrating)
A Mutation of Thrushes
A Nest of Vipers
A Nursery of Raccoons
A Nye of Pheasants
  ('A Bouquet' in flight; a pair is
  'A Brace')
An Obstinacy of Buffalo
A Pace of Donkeys
A Pack of Coyotes
A Pack of Dogs
A Pack of Stoats
A Pandemonium of Parrots
A Parade of Elephants
A Parcel of Linnets
A Parcel of Penguins
A Parliament of Owls
A Party of Jays
A Passel of Opossums

A Peep of Chickens
A Pile of Platypuses
A Pitying of Turtle Doves
A Plague of Locusts
A Pod of Birds (a small flock)
A Pod of Dolphins
A Prickle of Porcupines
A Pride of Lions
A Pungent of Sasquatch
A Quantity of Smelt
A Quiver of Cobras
A Rabble of Butterflies
A Raft of Sea Otters
A Rafter of Turkeys
  (a group of males is
  'A Posse')
A Rag of Colts
A Rhumba of Rattlesnakes
A Richness of Martens
A Rout of Snails
A Rout of Wolves
A Scattering of Herons
  ('A Heronry' for a large
  roosting group)
A Scourge of Mosquitoes
A Sedge of Bitterns
A Seething of Eels
A Shiver of Sharks
A Shoal of Fish
  (for a group of fish which has
  come together deliberately;
  'A School' is a tightly

organized group; a group that
happens to be together is 'An
Aggregation'; it is 'A Run'
when in motion and 'A Catch'
when fished unless caught by
net, in which case 'A Draught')
A Shoal of Octopuses
A Shrewdness of Apes
A Siege of Cranes
A Skulk of Foxes
A Sloth of Bears
A Smack of Jellyfish
A Sord of Mallards
A Sounder of Wild Boar
A Spring of Teal
A Steam of Minnows
A String of Ponies
A String of Racehorses
A Stud of Mares
A Surfeit of Skunks
A Sute of Bloodhounds
A Swarm of Grasshoppers
A Swarm of Lemmings
A Swarm of Moths
A Tittering of Magpies
A Tok of Capercailzies
A Tower of Giraffes
A Train of Camels
  ('A Caravan' when used as
  beasts of burden)
A Trip of Dotterel
A Trip of Goats

A Trip of Mice
A Trogle of Snakes
A Troop of Baboons
A Troop of Dogfish
A Troop of Kangaroos
A Troubling of Goldfish
  (*'A Run' when in motion*)
A Turn of Tortoises

A Turn of Turtles
An Unkindness of Ravens
A Wake of Buzzards
A Walk of Snipe
A Watch of Nightingales
A Whoop of Gorillas
A Wobble of Ostriches
A Zapper of Flycatchers

A MESS OF IGUANAS,
A WHOOP OF GORILLAS

AN AMBUSH OF TIGERS

♫ Tigers roar and growl.

🐾 White tigers are very rare in the wild and all zoo specimens descend from just two wild animals.

🐾 Tigers and lions are quite similar anatomically and can be interbred. The results are known as either ligers or tigons. A liger is the offspring of a male lion and a tigress and occurs naturally in the wild, however, a male liger is infertile.

🐾 Tigers are the largest species of the cat family. Some Siberian tigers reach 13ft (4m) long. Despite their incredible size they prefer fleeing to fighting but can leap as high as 5m and as far as 10m, making them one of the highest-jumping mammals.

🐾 There are only an estimated 7,000 wild tigers left. The majority of the world's tigers live in captivity. There are an estimated 12,000 tigers kept as pets in the US alone. Amazingly fifteen states require only a licence to own a tiger and sixteen states have no regulations at all.

🐾 Unfortunately they are poor climbers, taking to trees only in emergencies, but strong swimmers, happy to chase deer into the water.

🐾 The tiger's stripes are unique to each animal. The stripe pattern is found on a tiger's skin and if shaved, its distinctive camouflage pattern would be preserved.

3

AN ARMY OF ANTS

🐾 Amazon (and Polygerus) ants steal the larvae of other ants to keep as slaves. The slave ants build homes for and feed the Amazons who depend completely on their slaves for survival.

🐾 The sting of a jack jumper ant can be fatal. Bullet ants found in Central and South America have the most painful sting of any insect, according to the Schmidt Sting Pain Index.

🐾 There are at least 12,000 recorded species of ant currently living.

🐾 Ants have dominated most of the world's ecosystems for over 60 million years. Some scientists think that at least 15 per cent of the animal biomass of the world is made up of ants and termites.

🐾 Ants don't sleep much – a few minutes a day is more than enough.

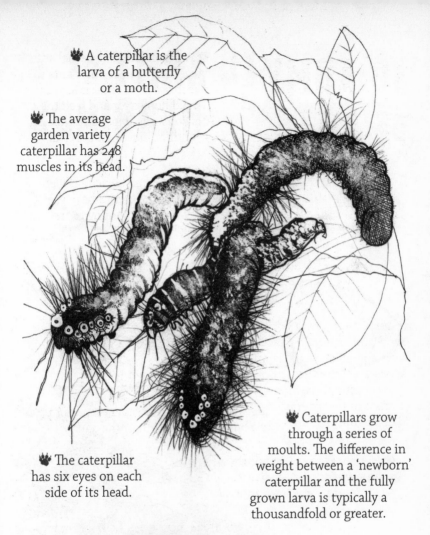

🐾 A caterpillar is the larva of a butterfly or a moth.

🐾 The average garden variety caterpillar has 248 muscles in its head.

🐾 The caterpillar has six eyes on each side of its head.

🐾 Caterpillars grow through a series of moults. The difference in weight between a 'newborn' caterpillar and the fully grown larva is typically a thousandfold or greater.

AN ARMY OF CATERPILLARS

AN ARMY OF HERRINGS

♫ Herrings use high frequency for communication
via bubbles coming out of the anus.

🐾 Herring is the most widely eaten fish
in the world and has been a known staple
food source since 3000 BC.

🐾 Unlike most other fish, herrings
have soft dorsal fins that lack spines.

🐾 Very young herrings are
called whitebait and are eaten
whole as a delicacy.

🐾 Hedgehogs were commonly eaten in Ancient Egypt and some recipes of the Late Middle Ages call for hedgehog meat. As recently as 2006, the UK newspaper the *Guardian* offered a recipe for hedgehog spaghetti carbonara which called for 250g lean hedgehog among the ingredients.

🐾 It was widely believed that hedgehogs sucked cows' udders, and old churchwardens' accounts record payments of a few pence per head for killing them.

AN ARRAY OF HEDGEHOGS

🐾 The name 'hedgehog' came into use around 1450, derived from the Middle English 'heyghoge', from 'heyg' or 'hegge' meaning hedge, because it frequents hedgerows, and 'hoge' meaning hog from its pig-like snout.

♫ Hedgehogs communicate in a series of grunts and snuffles and some species also emit loud squeals.

🐾 Hedgehogs have a high level of immunity to viper venom.

🐾 There are fossils of modern hedgehog ancestors dating back 70 million years, demonstrating that hedgehogs lived in the time of dinosaurs.

🐾 The skylark is known for the song of the male which is delivered in hovering flight from heights of up to 300ft.

🐾 The male skylark has broader wings than the female. This allows them to hover and sing for longer which is more attractive to the females.

🐾 The traditional French song 'Alouette' is a song about the plucking of a skylark, with alouette being the word for skylark.

AN ASCENSION OF SKYLARKS

AN ASYLUM OF CUCKOOS

🐾 The practice of laying its eggs in other birds' nests has resulted in the cuckoo being regarded as a symbol of unfaithfulness. However, in Japan the cuckoo is a symbol of unrequited love.

🐾 The mangrove cuckoo is totally silent except during the breeding season.

🐾 Spiny caterpillars account for a large part of the black-billed cuckoo's diet. The spines of the caterpillars stick in the lining of the bird's stomach. To remove the spines this cuckoo's stomach lining is periodically shed.

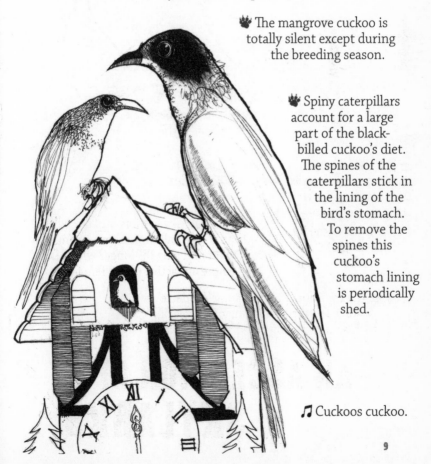

🎵 Cuckoos cuckoo.

AN ASYLUM
OF LOONS

🐾 During the mating season they use their bills and wings to 'crawl' on land.

♫ Loons howl. Their howl is best described as a yodel while their tremolo sound is likened to a crazy human laugh. This has resulted in a commonly used collective noun for them, particularly in the US, being 'a cry'.

🐾 Loons, as well as hummingbirds, swifts, kingfishers and grebes, are all birds that cannot walk well, if at all. The red-throated loon is the only loon that can take off from land.

🐾 All loons, other than the red-throated loon, carry their young on their back.

🐾 Unlike most bird species which have hollow bones, the loon has solid bones to aid diving. The common loon dives up to 200ft.

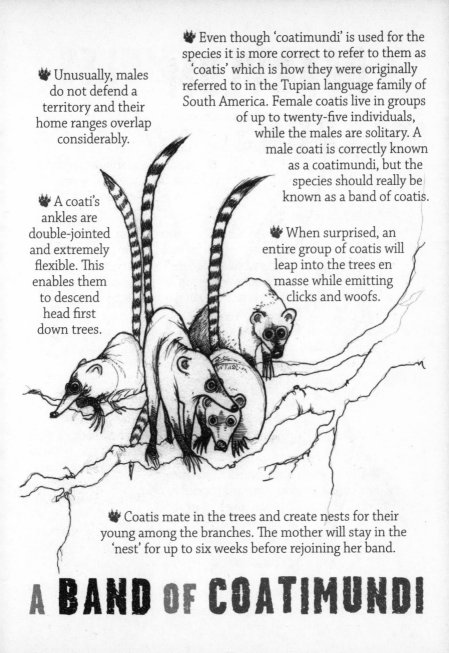

🐾 Even though 'coatimundi' is used for the species it is more correct to refer to them as 'coatis' which is how they were originally referred to in the Tupian language family of South America. Female coatis live in groups of up to twenty-five individuals, while the males are solitary. A male coati is correctly known as a coatimundi, but the species should really be known as a band of coatis.

🐾 Unusually, males do not defend a territory and their home ranges overlap considerably.

🐾 A coati's ankles are double-jointed and extremely flexible. This enables them to descend head first down trees.

🐾 When surprised, an entire group of coatis will leap into the trees en masse while emitting clicks and woofs.

🐾 Coatis mate in the trees and create nests for their young among the branches. The mother will stay in the 'nest' for up to six weeks before rejoining her band.

A BAND OF COATIMUNDI

A BARREN OF MULES

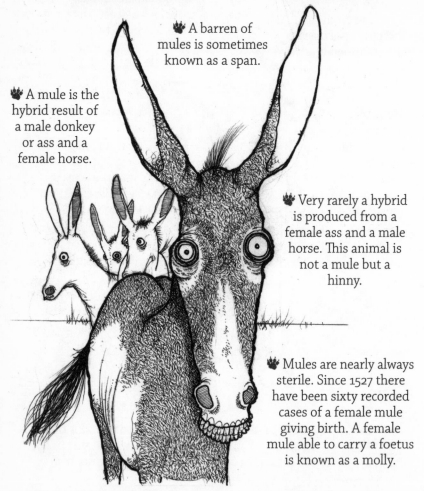

🐾 A barren of mules is sometimes known as a span.

🐾 A mule is the hybrid result of a male donkey or ass and a female horse.

🐾 Very rarely a hybrid is produced from a female ass and a male horse. This animal is not a mule but a hinny.

🐾 Mules are nearly always sterile. Since 1527 there have been sixty recorded cases of a female mule giving birth. A female mule able to carry a foetus is known as a molly.

🐾 After the American Civil War, freed African-American slaves were promised 40 acres and a mule.

🐾 Barracudas are known to store 'fresh' food. After finishing eating, a battery of barracudas may attempt to herd the shoal of fish they were eating into shallow water. The fish are then guarded until the barracuda are ready for their next meal.

🐾 Barracudas can live up to fourteen years of age. You can measure a barracuda's age by counting the rings on its scales or in a tiny structure called an otolith in its ear.

🐾 Great barracuda can grow up to 1.8m (6ft) long and swim in the Atlantic from Florida to Brazil.

A BATTERY
OF BARRACUDAS

🐾 Consuming barracuda is considerably more harmful to humans than eating any other fish species. Barracudas caught in tropical waters may be poisonous, causing a type of food poisoning in humans called ciguatera. The barracuda feed on fish which in turn feed on algae containing a toxin. One case where being at the top of a food chain doesn't pay off.

A BAZAAR OF FALCONS

🐾 The peregrine falcon primarily feeds on birds which it takes in mid-air, normally after a steep dive from above. The falcon's dive is known as a stoop, which doesn't seem to describe it at all.

🐾 The gyrfalcon was prized by falconers throughout history. In the Middle Ages only a king could hunt with a gyrfalcon.

🐾 The peregrine falcon is the fastest bird on record, at over 175mph when diving.

🐾 The merlin, a type of falcon, attacks other birds of prey to protect its territory. Popular in medieval falconry, the collective noun is an illusion of merlins.

🐾 Kestrels, a type of small falcon, are able to see near-ultraviolet light. This allows them to detect the urine trails around rodent burrows which reflect this ultraviolet light.

🐾 *The Boke of St Albans* provides a falconry hierarchy matching birds with the social rank that was considered appropriate for each bird. Under this system, an emperor should use an eagle, a king should use a gyrfalcon, peregrine falcons were for earls, priests should use sparrowhawks and the lowly knave had to make do with a kestrel.

🐾 Falconry, the sport of hunting with falcons,
as well as with hawks and birds of prey, has been
practised since the eighth century BC. It is believed that
a popular game played in the Middle Ages by nobility
and royalty, while waiting for the falcons to return,
was to come up with and create the collective nouns
of animals, many of which we still use today.

♫ Falcons chant.

🐾 The pigeon guillemot climbs vertical walls by using its sharp claws while flapping its wings.

A BAZAAR OF GUILLEMOTS

🐾 No other bird in the world breeds in such close proximity to its neighbours as the guillemot, with some birds pressed in shoulder to shoulder.

🐾 The guillemot breeds on narrow ledges on sheer cliffs. The egg they lay is cone-shaped which means it will roll in an arc and so is less likely to roll off the cliff.

🐾 Chicks jump into the sea from cliff ledges, before they know how to fly, in order to go to sea and feed with their father.

🐾 Guillemots can dive to great depths and have been recorded at the base of a North Sea oil rig at 292ft.

❧ It can take a deep-sea clam up to one hundred years to reach 0.3in (8mm) in length. The clam is among the slowest growing species in the world.

❧ Scottish razor clams can be easily harvested by hand by pouring salt or saltwater into their burrows. They confuse the salt with the rising tide and emerge from the sand.

❧ The clam is the longest living species on the planet. Some clams have been estimated to be over four hundred years old.

A BED OF CLAMS

A BED OF OYSTERS

🐾 Over her lifetime a female oyster may produce over 100 million young.

🐾 Oysters can change from one gender to another and back again depending on which is best for mating.

🐾 Left to their own devices, and without human intervention, pearls grow naturally only once in every 20,000 oysters.

🐾 Sadly it is a myth that oysters act as an aphrodisiac, though they are a rich source of zinc, one of the minerals required for the production of testosterone.

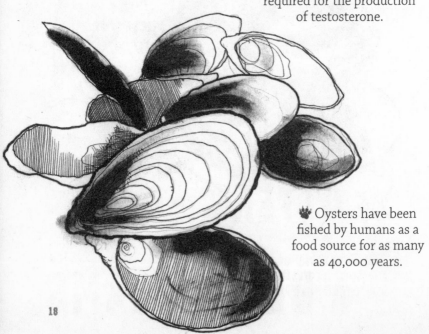

🐾 Oysters have been fished by humans as a food source for as many as 40,000 years.

A BEVY OF OTTERS

🐾 Otter droppings are known as spraints and have an odour similar to jasmine tea.

🐾 The word 'otter' has the same root as the words 'water' and 'wet'.

🐾 An otter's den is called a holt.

🐾 The giant otter of South America has a body up to 7ft long.

🐾 It is not recommended to try and kill a hornet anywhere near its nest as it will send out a distress signal which can trigger the entire nest to attack.

🐾 Hornets do not die after stinging and are able to sting multiple times.

A BIKE OF HORNETS

🐾 Hornets build their hives by chewing wood into a papery construction pulp.

🐾 There are over 15,000 species of wasps worldwide.

🐾 Wasps feed on sweet liquids. Some that have been observed feeding on fermenting juice eventually get drunk and pass out.

A BIKE OF WASPS

🐾 Only female wasps can sting.

🐾 Tarantula wasps have a wingspan of about 12cm. They paralyse tarantulas and lay a single egg on the still-living spider. When the egg hatches the wasp larva has fresh food.

🐾 The venom sac at the end of a wasp sting keeps pulsing for a short period after a wasp dies so a dead wasp may still sting you.

🐾 The world's smallest winged insect is the Tanzanian parasitic wasp. It is less than a tenth of a millimetre in size – smaller than the eye of a housefly.

🐾 The Ainu people of Japan taught dogs how to catch leaping salmon as they returned to their breeding grounds.

🐾 Wild Atlantic salmon can hurdle 12ft waterfalls.

A BIND OF SALMON

🐾 Wild Atlantic salmon can survive for up to twenty-two months without eating when they return from the ocean to their birth rivers.

🐾 Salmon have featured in mythology often with attributes of wisdom. The Welsh believed that the salmon of Llyn Llyw was the oldest animal in the world and was consulted by King Arthur and his knights.

🐾 The first laws regarding the fishing of the Atlantic salmon were started over 700 years ago by Edward I of England. Alexander II of Scotland followed this up in 1318 by outlawing salmon traps in rivers.

🐾 Wild Atlantic salmon were one of the earliest known art subjects. A life-size salmon was sculpted in a cave in south-west France almost 22,000 years ago.

🐾 For every million Atlantic salmon eggs spawned, one albino fish will be produced. Its chance of surviving in the wild is virtually nil.

🐾 An Irish tradition is that salmon gain wisdom by eating the nuts of hazel trees and the number of spots on a salmon's back shows how many nuts he's eaten.

A BLOAT OF
HIPPOPOTAMI
(OR HIPPOPOTAMUSES)

🐾 A hippopotamus can outrun a human.

🐾 Hippos are born underwater. The ears and nostrils of the hippo close automatically when it is submerged.

🐾 Despite many adaptations for life in the water, hippos can't swim or even float. They move by pushing off from the bottom of the river or by walking along the riverbed.

🐾 DNA evidence suggests that the hippopotamus is more closely related to whales and dolphins than it is to any other artiodactyl (even-toed hoofed mammal).

🐾 US President George Washington's false teeth were not made of wood, as is commonly believed, but were in fact carved from the tusks of a hippopotamus.

♫ Hippos bray.

A BOOGLE OF WEASELS

🐾 A boogle of weasels is more commonly known as a pack. Other collective nouns for weasels are a gang and a confusion.

🐾 The skunk-like zorilla, closely related to the weasel, is the smelliest animal on the planet. Its anal glands can be smelled from half a mile away. As a consequence it has very few enemies (and very few friends!).

🐾 Weasels have to eat one third of their body weight every twenty-four hours.

🐾 Weasels have a tough time. Due to their small size they make good prey for a wide range of predators including hawks, foxes, owls and cats. Only one in 80–90 weasels survives to over two years old.

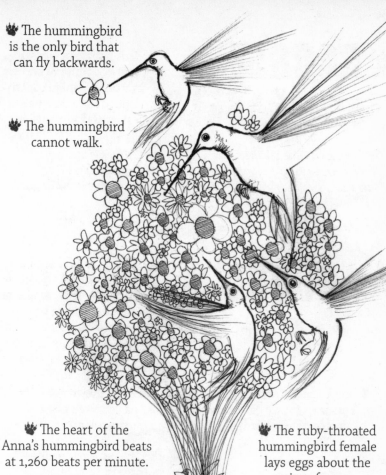

❦ The hummingbird is the only bird that can fly backwards.

❦ The hummingbird cannot walk.

❦ The heart of the Anna's hummingbird beats at 1,260 beats per minute.

❦ The ruby-throated hummingbird female lays eggs about the size of peas.

❦ The collective noun for a group of Lucifer hummingbirds is an inferno.

A BOUQUET OF HUMMINGBIRDS

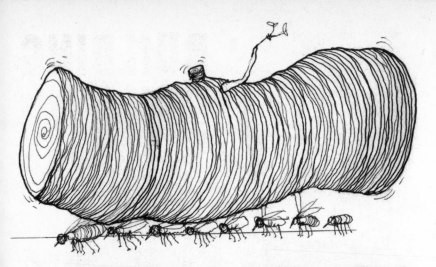

A BROOD OF TERMITES

🐾 Termite mounds can reach up to 40ft high.

🐾 Anteaters prefer termites to ants.

🐾 Some species of termite practise agriculture. They create well-planned fungal gardens which are fed on collected plant matter. These gardens provide food for the colony.

🐾 Worker and soldier termites are both sterile and blind.

🐾 Some soldier termites have mouths so large that they are unable to feed themselves.

🐾 Termites are a major source of one of the harmful greenhouse gases, atmospheric methane.

A BUILDING OF ROOKS

♫ Rooks caw.

🐾 Rooks nest in large colonies known as rookeries. A large rookery can contain up to 65,000 individuals.

🐾 A common but unpopular bird, by 1508 'rook' had also come to be used as a negative description of someone and by 1577 being called a rook meant you were 'a cheat' – particularly when gambling with cards and dice. By 1590 'to rook' was the verb used to mean 'to defraud by cheating'. By the end of the nineteenth century a raw recruit in the military became known as a rookie, supposedly because they were easy to cheat.

🐾 A group of ducks on water is known as a paddling of ducks. The collective noun for ducks in flight is a team.

🐾 The goosander is a species of duck that eats fish and is collectively known as a dopping.

🎵 Ducks quack.

🐾 Ducks on the outer edges of a group sleep with one eye open. Those in the centre of the group confidently close both eyes.

🐾 On the subject of quacking ducks, recent scientific tests have proved that it is a myth that a duck's quack does not echo. It does, it's just hard to hear as the quack fades out and the echo is confused with the original sound.

🐾 The collective noun for a widgeon, a species of freshwater duck, is a company.

🐾 Most domestic ducks are descended from the mallard, a species of wild duck. Their collective noun is a sord.

A BUNCH OF DUCKS

A BUNCH OF WILDFOWL OR WATERFOWL

🐾 A bunch of wildfowl is sometimes referred to as a plump. A bunch of waterfowl numbering less than thirty birds is called a knob.

🐾 Wildfowl is an Old English term for wild game birds, such as a wild ducks, goose or quail.

🐾 Waterfowl refers to traditional aquatic game birds such as ducks or swans.

🐾 A dense group of waterfowl is collectively known as a raft.

🐾 The hunting of any wildfowl or waterfowl is commonly known as duck hunting.

❧ Horseshoe crabs have existed in essentially the same form for the past 135 million years.

❧ The blood of the horseshoe crab provides a test for the toxins that cause septic shock, which previously led to 50 per cent of all hospital-acquired infections and 20 per cent of all hospital deaths. They are also used in finding remedies for diseases that have developed resistances to penicillin and other drugs while enzymes from their blood have been used by astronauts in the International Space Station to test surfaces for unwanted bacteria.

❧ The giant Japanese spider crab can grow to 12ft from claw tip to claw tip.

A BUSHEL OF CRABS

🐾 A female ferret will die if it goes into heat and cannot find a mate.

🐾 The male ferret is called a hob, the female a jill and their young are known as kittens.

🐾 Ferrets like to hoard objects, which is where the phrase 'to ferret away' comes from.

A BUSINESS OF FERRETS

🐾 The pet ferret was domesticated more than 500 years before the house cat. It was originally used by man for hunting or ferreting for small mammals such as rabbits.

🐾 The ferret's Latin name, *Mustela putorius furo*, translates as 'mouse-catching stinky thief'.

🐾 When ferrets are happy and excited, they may perform a routine commonly referred to as 'the weasel war dance' which is often accompanied by a soft clucking noise, commonly referred to as dooking.

🐾 Trained ferrets have been used to run wires and cables through large conduits. Perhaps their most high-profile 'job' was laying the TV and sound cables for the wedding of Prince Charles to Lady Diana Spencer.

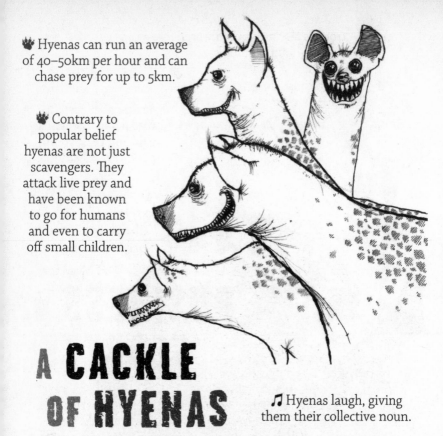

🐾 Hyenas can run an average of 40–50km per hour and can chase prey for up to 5km.

🐾 Contrary to popular belief hyenas are not just scavengers. They attack live prey and have been known to go for humans and even to carry off small children.

A CACKLE OF HYENAS

♫ Hyenas laugh, giving them their collective noun.

🐾 Hyenas are capable of eating and digesting their entire prey, including teeth, skin, horns and bones.

🐾 In Ancient Egypt hyenas were domesticated and raised for food.

🐾 Hyenas are very intelligent and hyena society is similar to that of the baboon in terms of complexity, recognition of individuals, and social hierarchy.

🐾 Hyenas have been known to hide prey underwater to cover the scent. They are careful to avoid crocodile infested water.

🐾 A troop is also a commonly used collective noun for monkeys.

🐾 The first monkey in space was Albert II who flew in the US-launched V2 rocket in 1949. A Rhesus macaque called Sam was flown to a height of 55 miles in 1959.

🐾 Howler monkeys are the noisiest land animals. Their calls can be heard over 2 miles away.

🐾 The nose of Borneo's proboscis monkey can grow to 20cm long.

♫ Monkeys chatter and gibber.

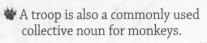

A CARTLOAD OF MONKEYS

A CETE of BADGERS

🐾 A cete is often written as a 'set' and was first recorded with badgers in *The Boke of St Albans* in 1486 although it was used as early as the 1440s to mean a 'collection of things'.

🐾 The badger is the best digger of all meat-eating or carnivorous mammals.

🐾 The dachshund was originally bred in Germany to hunt badgers. The German word for badger is 'dachs'.

🐾 Badgers were one of the primary meat sources for the Native Americans and are still eaten in many parts of the world including China and Russia, and used in some rural French dishes. Badgers were last legally eaten in the UK during the Second World War.

🐾 Bobolinks like to eat cultivated grains and rice.

♫ Bobolinks chek.

🐾 The bobolink migration every autumn is a round trip of approximately 20,000 km.

🐾 The bobolink is one of the few songbirds that undergoes two complete moults each year. It completely changes its feathers on both the breeding and wintering grounds.

A CHAIN OF BOBOLINKS

🐾 After mating, the male bobolink changes feather colouring from the black and white 'evening dress' of courtship to the camouflaged plumage in which he will spend the rest of the year.

🐾 In Jamaica the bobolink is considered a delicacy and is known as the butter bird.

🐾 Goldfinches sometimes decorate the outside of their nests with aromatic flowers.

🐾 The canary, a type of finch, was the first songbird to be domesticated and kept as a cage-bird. Following the conquest of the Canary Islands by the Spanish in 1478 the trade in canaries swept Europe.

🐾 Groups of most finches are correctly called charms. However, in the case of the linnet a parcel is the true term.

🐾 Half the known species of bird in the world belong to the finch family, including the sparrow, the weaver bird and the cardinal.

A CHARM
OF GOLDFINCHES

A CHATTER OF BUDGERIGARS

🐾 Budgerigar plumage is known to fluoresce under ultraviolet light.

🐾 Chocolate, avocado and alcohol are extremely toxic to budgerigars.

🐾 A budgerigar named Puck who died in America in 1994 holds the world record for the largest vocabulary of any bird, at 1,728 words.

🐾 Budgerigar means 'good eating' in some Australian Aboriginal languages.

A CHATTERING OF CHOUGHS

🐾 Choughs are known as balores in Cornwall and have become the emblem for Cornish cultural identity.

🐾 Intruders into chough territory are often dive-bombed by the entire chattering.

🐾 Choughs sometimes kidnap juveniles from other groups to make their own groups larger.

A CLOUD OF CRICKETS

🎵 Only full-grown male crickets can chirp. They have four distinct songs: a calling song to signal to females; a soft courting song when a female is near; a copulatory song following successful mating; and an aggressive song when a rival male is detected nearby.

🐾 To hear, the cricket uses ears located on its knees.

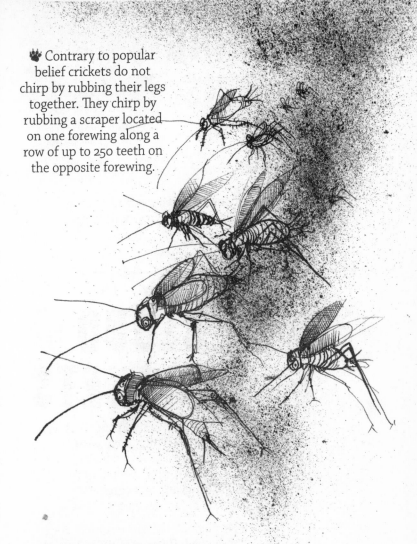

Contrary to popular belief crickets do not chirp by rubbing their legs together. They chirp by rubbing a scraper located on one forewing along a row of up to 250 teeth on the opposite forewing.

Crickets are omnivores and will even resort to cannibalism of their own dead when no other food is available.

🐾 Flies have 4,000 lenses in each eye – yet they still have poor vision.

🐾 Flies jump up and backwards when taking off.

🐾 Flies spread bacteria every time they land. They are also capable of spreading anthrax, dysentery, cholera, TB, gangrene, leprosy, scarlet fever, yellow fever and bubonic plague to humans.

A CLOUD OF FLIES

🐾 The bot fly shoots its eggs directly into the eyes of sheep where the maggots hatch. There are documented cases of these flies mistaking humans for sheep and turning the unfortunate person into an incubator.

🐾 A group of flies is also known as a business of flies.

🐾 There are over 120,000 species of fly.

♫ Flies buzz. Apparently common house flies hum in the key of F.

🐾 Flies are the only insects that have only two wings – all other insects have four.

🐾 The house fly beats its wings over 20,000 times a minute.

🐾 Flies don't grow. They are born full size.

A CLOUD OF GNATS

🐾 A large cloud of male gnats assembled in a mating swarm is known as a ghost.

🐾 The First World War poet Rupert Brooke was killed as a result of a gnat bite.

🐾 The male gnat does not have piercing jaws – only the female is able to draw blood.

A CLOWDER OF

🐾 A group of kittens is called a kindle.

🐾 A 'cloudyr of cattys' was first recorded in *The Egerton Manuscript* of 1450 while *The Boke of St Albans* of 1486 records 'a kyndyll of yong cattis'.

🎵 Cats meow, mew, purr and caterwaul.

🐾 A cat will almost never meow at another cat. Cats use this sound for humans.

🐾 Current domestic cats were the result of genetic mutation which was exploited through breeding so that they would be tame at birth.

🐾 The collective noun for wild cats is a destruction.

🐾 The only domestic animal not mentioned in the Bible is the cat.

🐾 In 1888, an estimated 300,000 mummified cats were found at Beni Hassan, Egypt. They were sold at $18.43 per ton, and shipped to England to be ground up and used for fertilizer.

🐾 Cats step with both left legs, then both right legs when they walk or run. The only other animals to do this are the giraffe and the camel.

🐾 When the Black Death swept across England in the fourteenth century, one theory was that cats caused the plague, and many thousands were slaughtered. Households that kept their cats were less affected, because they kept their houses clear of the real culprits, rats.

CATS

🐾 Unlike the antlers of deer, antelope horns are made of bone.

🐾 The word antelope comes from the Byzantine Greek and was first recorded in the fourth century AD by Eustathius of Antioch and referred to a hard to catch animal with saw-like horns that inhabited the banks of the Euphrates. The word was first used in 1607 to describe the various species of antelopes known at the time.

🐾 Gazelle-sized antelope often leap while being chased. This is known as pronking or stotting and signifies to the predator, who would normally hunt a sick or old animal, that the potential prey is in good health and so less likely to be caught.

🐾 Deer species are very varied. The diminutive royal antelope only stands at 24cm at the shoulder while the Kudu can jump 2m in the air from a standing start.

A **CLUSTER** OF **ANTELOPE**

🐾 The eland is the heaviest antelope and can reach 1 ton in weight.

A CLUSTER
OF MUSSELS

🐾 Despite cluster being correct, the commonly used collective noun for mussels is a bed. Strictly speaking a bed is the place where mussels grow together. This has resulted in fishermen who deal in groups of mussels adopting a bed as their own collective noun.

🐾 Mussels exhibit cannibalistic behaviour. At certain times of the year, up to 70 per cent of all food eaten by the green-lipped mussel is the larvae of its own species.

🐾 Mussels are a rich source of iodine, protein, iron, copper and selenium, and a good source of calcium, vitamin B2 and niacin. They are also a source of zinc.

🐾 Mussels are able to move slowly by means of a muscular foot.

🐾 Zebra mussels are also believed to be the source of deadly avian botulism poisoning that has resulted in the death of tens of thousands of birds in the Great Lakes of North America since the late 1990s.

🐾 Mussels feed and breathe by filtering water through extensible tubes called siphons. A large mussel filters up to 38l of water per day.

🐾 Spiders don't only have eight legs.
Most species also have eight eyes.

🐾 The world's oldest preserved spider
web was found in Spain, preserved in
110-million-year-old amber.

🐾 Tarantula hair is
the main ingredient
in the novelty item
itching powder.

🐾 Some species of social spiders
build communal webs that may
house up to 50,000 individuals.

A CLUSTER OF SPIDERS

🐾 Spiders lack balance
and rely on their eyes to tell
them which way is up.

🐾 Spiders use hydraulic pressure to extend their
limbs which is why a dead spider's legs curl up.

🐾 Bolas spiders make a bolas from a single
thread with a sticky ball at the end. These bolas emit
a chemical similar to the pheromone of a moth to
attract prey. They swing the bolas at the prey and
succeed in catching a moth in 50 per cent of strikes.

🐾 Cooked tarantula is a delicacy in Cambodia.

🐾 The water spider spends its life underwater.
Using a dense mat of specialized hairs that covers its body
and abdomen it traps a bubble of air around its body.

🐾 The zebra spider is believed to have the
best eyesight of any arthropod. It will often
turn its head to look straight back at you.

A COALITION OF CHEETAHS

♫ Cheetahs chirp. The sound is similar to a bird's chirp or a dog's yelp and can be heard a mile away. They also growl, hiss and snarl as well as engaging in churring and purring.

🐾 The name cheetah comes from the Hindi word 'chita' meaning 'spotted one'.

🐾 The cheetah is the only cat in the world that can't retract its claws.

🐾 The modern cheetah population can be traced back to a single African group of 500 animals that survived the last ice age.

🐾 Cheetahs were trained by man for hunting as long ago as 3000 BC. Kept by the likes of the Ancient Egyptians, Akbar the Great, Genghis Khan and Charlemagne, cheetahs were used as hunting animals in India until the mid twentieth century and as recently as the 1930s the Emperor Haile Selassie of Ethiopia was often photographed leading a pet cheetah by a lead.

❧ The leg bones of a bat are so thin that most bats cannot walk.

❧ There are an estimated 1,100 species of bat accounting for about 20 per cent of all mammal species.

❧ Bats almost always turn left when leaving a cave.

❧ The world's smallest mammal is the bumblebee bat of Thailand, weighing in at around 2g.

❧ The tube-lipped nectar bat of Ecuador has the longest tongue of any animal relative to its body size. It evolved alongside a bell-shaped flower and is now the only creature capable of pollinating it.

A COLONY OF BATS

❧ Bats rarely fly in the rain as it interferes with their echo location, making them unable to locate food.

❧ Most cases of rabies reported in humans come from bats. Despite this, over 99 per cent of bats do not carry rabies.

🐾 Chinchillas' natural habitat is the high Andes of Chile and Bolivia but sadly hunting has made them scarce in the wild. Nearly all living chinchillas are bred for their fur and are descended from a small colony introduced into the US in 1923. Even organizing this was no easy task, as after three years of searching only eleven animals had been found and it took a further twelve months to bring them down the 12,000ft mountain as they had to acclimatize to the altitude as they went.

A COLONY OF CHINCHILLAS

♫ Chinchillas chirp, squeak and bark.

🐾 Chinchilla means 'little Chincha' and is named after the Chincha people of the Andes who wore its fur until it became more valuable to sell than to wear in the nineteenth century.

🐾 Prior to intensive fur 'farming' the rarity of the chinchilla meant that some designer coats would sell for up to $100,000.

🐾 If frightened, the female chinchilla may spray the offender with urine.

A COLONY of RATS

🐾 A group of rats is also
known as a pack or a swarm.

🐾 It has been estimated that nearly one quarter of all electric
cable breaks, phone cable disruptions and fires of unknown
origin are caused by rats. Apparently rats destroy an estimated
one third of the world's food supply each year. This makes the rat
the world's most destructive mammal other than man.

🐾 Rats are omnivorous, eating nearly
any type of food, including dead
and dying members of their
own species.

🐾 Rats multiply so
quickly that in
eighteen months,
two rats could have
over a million
descendants.

🐾 Plague did not
originate in rats.
It is believed that rats
contracted the plague
from the Mongolian
marmot.

🐾 A rat can swim
continuously for
seventy-two hours.

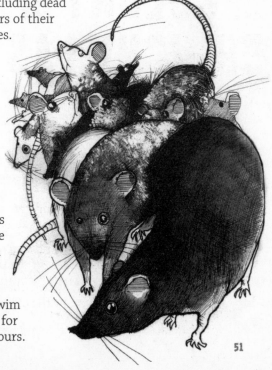

51

A COLONY OF

🐾 Corals form colonies by budding. These colonies in turn 'bud' to form reefs. A reef consists mainly of calcium carbonate, formed by the secretions of these small marine animals.

🐾 Coral is not only a living creature, related to the sea anemone, but is also the name used to refer to its skeleton.

🐾 Ancient coral reefs found on land where water has receded are commonly used as a building block material in East Africa known as 'coral rag'.

🐾 Corals reproduce by means of eggs and sperm. Coral larva attaches itself to a surface and secretes a skeleton, eventually becoming the parent of a new colony.

🐾 Current scientific estimates are that approximately 10 per cent of the world's coral reefs are already dead.

🐾 Indonesian waters contain nearly 33,000 square miles of coral reefs and are home to a third of the world's total corals and a quarter of its fish species. A recent study showed that less than 6 per cent of Indonesia's coral reefs are in excellent condition.

🐾 The Coral Triangle is an area around the waters of Indonesia, Timor-Leste, Malaysia, Papua New Guinea, the Philippines and the Solomon Islands and contains 75 per cent of all coral reef building corals in the world.

🐾 Australia's Great Barrier Reef is the world's biggest single structure made by living organisms. It is the largest deposit of coral in the world, extending for about 1,250 miles with an area of over 135,000 square miles. The largest of the UNESCO World Heritage Areas, the Reef can be seen from space.

🐾 The Great Barrier Reef first became known to Europeans when James Cook's *Endeavour* ran aground there on 11 June 1770.

CORALS

A group of vultures circling in the air is called a kettle.

A committee of vultures is sometimes referred to as a venue of vultures.

Vultures have weak claws and legs, and cannot attack or lift their prey.

Vultures mate for life.

A COMMITTEE OF VULTURES

Black vultures regurgitate when confronted.

Often vultures gorge so much they can't fly.

By eating rotting, putrefying carcasses, vultures stop the spread of disease, but never get ill themselves.

Vultures lack sweat glands and so they cool off by urinating.

The American turkey vulture helps human engineers detect cracked or broken underground fuel pipes. The leaking fuel smells like carrion and the clustered birds show where the lines need fixing.

A CONFUSION OF GUINEA FOWL

♫ Guinea fowl cry.

🐾 Guinea fowl are very good runners and use this method over flying as a way to escape predators.

🐾 Guinea fowl sold in Europe in the sixteenth century by Turkish traders were the reason that confused colonists in the Americas named the popular local bird a 'turkey'. This is also the origin of the guinea fowl's collective term.

A CONGREGATION

🐾 The live crocodile at Crocodilopolis in Ancient Egypt which was worshipped as a manifestation of the Egyptian god Sobek was named Petsuchos by the Greeks.

🐾 As the crocodile's jaw has evolved for biting down they are unable to open their mouths if held shut.

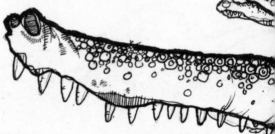

🎵 Crocodiles have well-developed vocal communication including bellows, snarls and grunts.

🐾 They have the strongest bite of any animal. The crocodile's bite force is more than 5,000lb per square inch (psi), compared to just 690 psi for a large great white shark and 800 psi for a hyena.

🐾 A crocodile can't move its tongue and cannot chew. Its digestive juices are so strong that it can digest a steel nail.

# of CROCODILES

🐾 Constant warning of the danger posed to man from the hippopotamus has, as of 2001, resulted in crocodiles becoming the leading cause of animal-related deaths (excluding mosquitoes).

🐾 A congregation of eagles is sometimes known as a convocation.

🎵 Eagles scream.

🐾 Eagles' nests are added to year after year and can become enormous, measuring up to 10ft across and weighing well over 1,000lb.

🐾 Eagles have been a symbol of war and power since Babylonian times.

🐾 The extinct Haast's eagle of New Zealand had a 3m wingspan and was the top predator in the archipelago's ecosystem prior to the arrival of humans.

A CONGREGATION OF EAGLES

🐾 In Kazakhstan and Mongolia, the golden eagle is used for hunting game as large as the fox.

🐾 Many eagle species lay two eggs, but the larger chick often kills its younger sibling once it has hatched. This takes 'survival of the fittest' to the extreme and hasn't helped eagle numbers soar.

A CONGREGATION OF PLOVERS

🐾 A congregation of plovers in flight is known as a wing.

🐾 The American golden plover flies up to 20,000 miles per year. They store seeds in their digestive tract to help sustain them during these flights.

🐾 If a predator approaches its nest, the common ringed plover will feign a broken wing to lure the intruder away from the eggs or young.

🐾 The collective noun for a dotterel, a rare Eurasian plover, is a trip.

A CONTRADICTION OF SANDPIPERS

🐾 Stilt sandpipers nest as close as 12ft to other shorebirds. However to protect the survival of their own species from predators they nest up to 900ft from fellow stilt sandpipers.

🐾 The spotted, solitary, Baird's, least, western, white-rumped and semipalmated sandpipers are collectively known as 'peeps'. The collective noun for peeps is a litter.

🎵 Sandpipers pipe and whistle.

🐾 The collective noun for a dunlin, a type of sandpiper, is a fling.

59

A COVERT OF COOTS

🐾 Coots are kleptoparasitic. When they don't feel like hunting for their own food, they'll steal from other birds.

🐾 If food becomes scarce, the young birds may be killed by their parents or other adults.

🐾 The coot is aggressive towards other water birds.

🐾 The collective noun for a group of coots when swimming is a shoal.

A COVEY OF GROUSE

🐾 The toes of ruffed grouse grow projections off their sides in winter. These projections act as snowshoes to help the grouse walk across snow.

🐾 In the mountains of Honshu, Japan, the ptarmigan is supposed to protect people and buildings from fire and thunder.

🎵 Grouse drum.

🐾 Historically important as a game bird, the grouse has several commonly used collective nouns including a chorus, drumming, grumbling and leash.

🐾 The white-tailed ptarmigan has feathers around its nostrils so that the air it breathes in is warmed before it reaches its body. The collective noun for a group of ptarmigan is an invisibleness of ptarmigan.

🐾 The capercailzie grouse found in northern Europe is commonly known as the cock of the woods and horse of the wood. Their collective noun is a tok of capercailzies.

A COVEY OF PARTRIDGES

🐾 Grey partridge hens produce some
of the largest clutches of any bird species,
with up to twenty-two eggs.

🐾 A partridge is a ground bird and so
very unlikely to be found in a pear tree.

A COVEY OF QUAILS

🐾 The top-knot that quails
have is called a hmuh.

🐾 Adult quails that engage in communal
brooding live longer than adults that do not.

🐾 The scaled quail normally roosts
tail-to-tail in a tight circle on the ground.

🐾 The smallest rhino species is the Sumatran rhino which weighs in at 1 ton, has a hairy coat and emits a distinctive whistle.

🐾 Rhino horns are made up of keratin, the same type of protein that makes up hair and fingernails.

🐾 The plural of rhinoceros can be rhinoceros, rhinoceri or rhinoceroses. They are commonly known as the rhino.

A CRASH OF RHINOCEROSES

🐾 The black rhino is similar in colour to the white rhino but was named black to distinguish the species. This is not helpful to an average spotter of rhinos.

🐾 The black rhino has eighty-four chromosomes. This is the highest known chromosome count for any mammal.

🐾 Black and white rhinos shared a common ancestor 4 million years ago and remain so closely related that they can still mate and successfully produce offspring.

🐾 An early ancestor of the rhino was Indricotherium, believed to be one of the largest land mammals that ever existed. The hornless animal was almost 7m high, 10m long, and weighed as much as 15 tons.

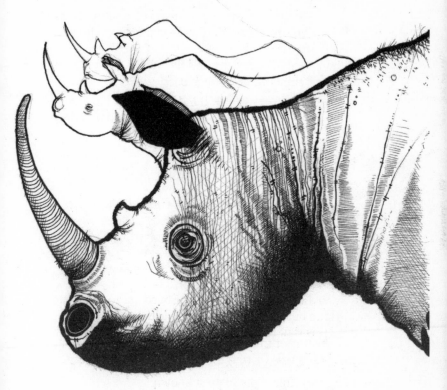

🐾 An adult white rhino can weigh up to 4 tons.

🎵 Rhinos snort.

A CRY OF HOUNDS

🐾 Hounds are dogs bred to hunt animals.
There are two main types: those that use ground
scent and airborne scent such as the basset; and
those that hunt by sight such as the Afghan.

🐾 The Afghan hound has been
used to hunt leopard in India.

🐾 The Afghan hound is among
the breeds of dog with the least
genetic divergence from the wolf.

🐾 In 2005 an Afghan hound called Snuppy entered the
record books as the first dog to be cloned. He was created
using the cell from an ear of an adult and involved 123
surrogate mothers, of which only three produced pups and of
these three he was the only survivor. Snuppy was named
Time magazine's 'Most Amazing Invention' of the year.

🐾 A couple and a half is the collective noun for a cry
consisting of three hounds, as recorded in the *Noble
Art of Venerie* written by George Turberville in 1575.

🐾 In the nineteenth century whippet
racing was a national sport in England and
was more popular than soccer.

🐾 The oldest known breed of domestic dog is the
Saluki whose relationship with man can be said to date
to 7000 BC. The Saluki was used to hunt gazelle.

🐾 A bloodhound can distinguish and identify several scents at the same time. The bloodhound is the only animal whose evidence is admissible in an American court. The collective noun for bloodhounds is a sute.

A CULTURE OF BACTERIA

🐾 There are an estimated 5 million trillion trillion bacteria on Earth. Technically speaking that is 5 nonillion bacteria or $5×10^{30}$.

🐾 Bacteria were the only form of life on Earth for 2 billion years.

🐾 Bacteria are found in the bodies of all living organisms and on every part of the Earth including Arctic ice, hot springs and the stratosphere.

🐾 The first person to observe and describe bacteria was the Dutch naturalist Anton van Leeuwenhoek in 1676.

🐾 Bacteria that are beneficial to humans far outnumber harmful varieties.

🐾 There are on average a million bacterial cells in a millilitre of fresh water.

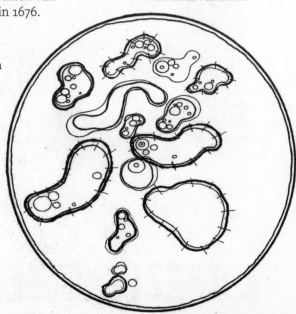

🐾 The different species of zebras do not interbreed. However, a zebdonk is a cross between a Burchell's zebra and a donkey.

🐾 A group of zebras is sometimes known as a herd, a cohort or a zeal.

🐾 Zebras sleep standing up and will only sleep when neighbours are around to warn them of predators.

🐾 Zebras are capable of running up to 40mph.

🐾 Every zebra has a unique pattern of stripes.

♫ Zebras communicate with each other with a high-pitched barking vocalization and make a whinny sound similar to a donkey.

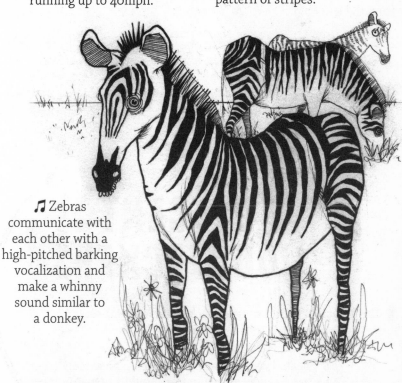

A DAZZLE OF ZEBRAS

A DECEIT OF LAPWINGS

🐾 A deceit of lapwings is often mistakenly called a desert. This in turn has been misspelled as 'dessert' and this can be found in some of the most respectable reference books.

🐾 The lapwing has an irregular flight pattern and the word lapwing is derived from the Old English verb for 'to totter'.

🐾 A lapwing will flap one wing when on the ground in order to pretend to have a broken wing in an attempt to lure predators away from its nest. This deceit is the original influence for its collective noun.

🐾 In the Netherlands there is a cultural-historical competition to find the first lapwing egg of the year.

A DESCENT OF WOODPECKERS

🐾 The tongue of the green woodpecker can reach 10cm. It is so long that it has to be curled round its skull.

🐾 Pileated woodpeckers will make up to sixteen holes in a tree to allow escape routes should a predator enter. They also peck the bark around the entrance holes to make the sap run from the tree to stop some predators, such as snakes, from entering the nest.

🐾 Some woodpeckers can strike a tree up to 150 times in a minute.

🐾 Just before the woodpecker's beak makes contact with wood a thickened nictitating membrane closes over the eye, protecting it from flying debris.

🐾 Woodpeckers can walk vertically up a tree.

🐾 A squirrel has no colour vision. It sees only in black and white. Unlike humans, whose focus is straight ahead, every part of a squirrel's field of vision is in perfect focus.

🐾 Millions of trees are accidentally planted by squirrels that bury nuts and then forget where they hid them.

🐾 The word squirrel was first recorded in 1327 and comes from the Anglo-Norman word 'esquirel' and the Old French 'escurel'.

🐾 Fairy tale heroine Cinderella originally wore squirrel fur slippers, known in French as 'vair'. The glass slipper that has become part of the story is a mistranslation from the similar sounding 'verre' meaning 'glass'. This is one of the most hotly debated fairy tale issues.

🐾 Squirrels climbing onto transformers and power lines while looking for food have been electrocuted and caused power blackouts. Squirrels have twice been responsible for bringing down the high-tech NASDAQ stock market.

🐾 Tree squirrels always descend head first.

🐾 Squirrels are immune to rabies.

A DRAY OF SQUIRRELS

A DULE OF DOVES

🐾 A pair of doves is known as a duet.

🎵 Doves coo and moan.

🐾 The collective noun for turtle doves is a pitying.

🐾 Turtle doves are considered emblems of devoted love.

🐾 A dule of doves is sometimes referred to as a dole of doves. Both are correct.

♫ Although best known for mimicking insect sound, birdsong and amphibian sound, mockingbirds can imitate a wide range of sounds, from a squeaking door to a cat meowing.

AN ECHO OF MOCKINGBIRDS

🐾 The blue mockingbird native to Mexico does not mimic the songs of other species.

🐾 It was after seeing various species of mockingbirds in the Galapagos Islands that Charles Darwin first recorded the expression of his doubts about species being unchangeable.

AN EXALTATION OF LARKS

🐾 The horned lark returns to its exact birthplace after every migration.

🐾 The male meadowlark usually has two mates on the go at the same time. The male is no romantic when it comes to rearing the young, leaving the females to do all the incubation and most of the feeding.

🐾 Larks are good at mimicking other bird whistles. They have also been known to imitate a shepherd's whistle so accurately that sheepdogs obey the signals as if their shepherd had given them.

🐾 The tiny feathers located at the first joint of the woodcock's wings are known as 'pin feathers' and are much in demand for artists brushes used for fine painting work.

🐾 Woodcocks may eat twice their weight in earthworms every day. They drum their feet to entice the worms to the surface where they are then extracted and eaten.

🐾 The woodcock's eyes are on the side of the head giving an almost 360° field of vision.

A FALL OF WOODCOCKS

🐾 The American woodcock has an elaborate courtship ritual that may be repeated once a month for as long as four consecutive months, continuing even after the females have already hatched their brood and left the nest. Despite this initial display of interest, there is no further bond between the pair and the male provides no care for the young.

🐾 Beaver fur was once the most valuable as it had waterproof qualities.

🐾 Infant beavers are called kittens.

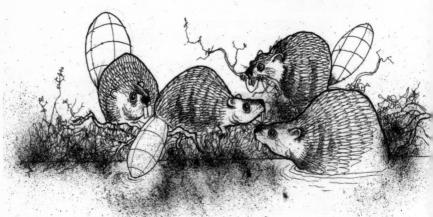

A FAMILY OF BEAVERS

🐾 In 1638, King Charles I decreed that all fur hats manufactured in England be made of North American beaver. This caused a series of beaver wars between the Iroquois with their English allies and the French with their Native American allies.

🐾 The beaver's instinct to build a dam leads wild beavers to 'reinforce' man-made dams and captive beavers often build dams that have no purpose.

A FAMILY OF SARDINES

🐾 Sardines are named after the island of Sardinia in whose waters they were once plentiful.

🐾 Sardines over 4in in length are known as pilchards.

🐾 South Africa's annual 'great sardine run' is one of the planet's great natural wonders. Every year, hundreds of millions of the fish leave Africa's most southerly point, Cape Agulhas, and swim north towards the beaches of KwaZulu-Natal. Shoals can be 7km long, 1.5km wide and 30m deep and attract huge numbers of predators with as many as 18,000 dolphins, sharks and whales in pursuit.

A FLAMBOYANCE OF FLAMINGOES

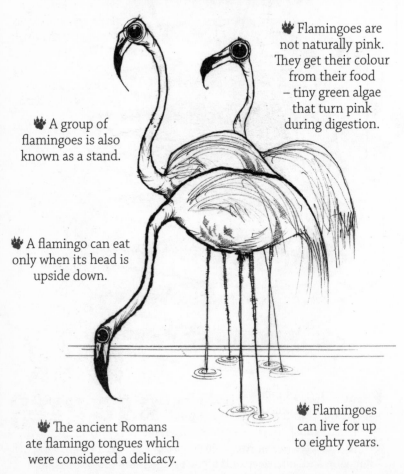

🐾 Flamingoes are not naturally pink. They get their colour from their food – tiny green algae that turn pink during digestion.

🐾 A group of flamingoes is also known as a stand.

🐾 A flamingo can eat only when its head is upside down.

🐾 The ancient Romans ate flamingo tongues which were considered a delicacy.

🐾 Flamingoes can live for up to eighty years.

🐾 A flick of domestic rabbits is known as a herd.

🐾 Mel Blanc, the voice of Bugs Bunny, was allergic to carrots. Although referred to as a rabbit, the drawing of Bugs Bunny is based on a hare.

🐾 A group of young rabbits is known as a kindle.

A FLICK OF RABBITS

🐾 The farming of rabbits for food is called cuniculture.

🐾 The only two animals that can see behind themselves without turning their heads are the rabbit and the parrot.

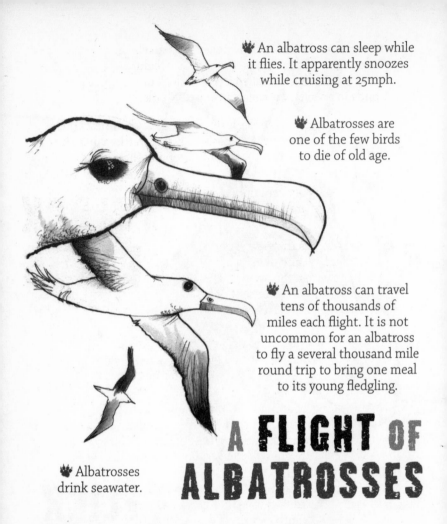

🐾 An albatross can sleep while it flies. It apparently snoozes while cruising at 25mph.

🐾 Albatrosses are one of the few birds to die of old age.

🐾 An albatross can travel tens of thousands of miles each flight. It is not uncommon for an albatross to fly a several thousand mile round trip to bring one meal to its young fledgling.

A **FLIGHT** OF **ALBATROSSES**

🐾 Albatrosses drink seawater.

🐾 Aided by its wingspan of up to 14ft, the albatross only needs to land once every couple of years to breed. The rest of the time it can roam the seas.

🐾 During the course of a fifty-year period an albatross can fly in excess of 3.5 million miles.

🐾 A group of birds is also known as a parcel. A flock of birds in the air is known as a flight and a small flock is called a pod. A flock of birds in an aviary is called a volary of birds.

🐾 Birds do not sleep in their nests. They may occasionally nap in them, but they actually sleep in other places.

♫ Birds sing.

🐾 95 per cent of bird species are monogamous.

A FLOCK OF BIRDS

🐾 Peru has the greatest biodiversity and density of birds with 1,780 species representing 18.5 per cent of all bird species on Earth.

🐾 It was a common belief among primitive tribes that the souls of the dead were conveyed to their afterlife by birds.

🐾 The longest annual bird migration is that of the sooty shearwaters, which nest in New Zealand and Chile and spend the summer feeding in the North Pacific, an annual round trip of 64,000km.

🐾 Guano (bird droppings) is a valuable fertilizer and has caused wars and slavery as recently as the late nineteenth century. From 1841 until the 1880s 80 per cent of Peru's foreign exchange came from selling guano.

🐾 The kiwi, the national bird of New Zealand, can't fly. It lives in a hole in the ground, is almost blind, hunts by smell and lays only one egg each year. Despite this, it has survived for more than 70 million years.

🐾 Flocks of blackbirds may contain up to 5 million birds.

🐾 The name 'blackbird' was first recorded in 1486.

🐾 The domestic cat is the main predator of the blackbird.

♫ Blackbirds whistle.

A FLOCK OF BLACKBIRDS

🐾 In medieval times it was considered entertaining to place live blackbirds under a pie crust so as to amuse one's guests. This practice is the origin of the nursery rhyme 'Sing a Song of Sixpence'.

🐾 Lice is the plural of louse and the term flock in relation to lice was first used by William Caxton in 1476.

🐾 There are over 3,300 species of lice and lice are parasites of every mammalian and avian order, with the notable exceptions of Monotremata (the platypus and the spiny anteater) and Chiroptera (bats).

🐾 As many a schoolchild will know, a louse egg is commonly called a nit. Lice attach their eggs to their host's hair with specialized saliva which results in a bond that is very difficult to separate without specialized products.

🐾 Recent DNA evidence suggests that pubic lice spread to the ancestors of humans *c.* 3.3 million years ago from the ancestors of gorillas by sharing the same bed or other communal areas with them.

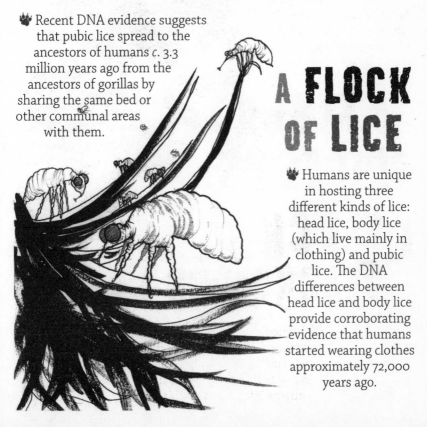

A FLOCK OF LICE

🐾 Humans are unique in hosting three different kinds of lice: head lice, body lice (which live mainly in clothing) and pubic lice. The DNA differences between head lice and body lice provide corroborating evidence that humans started wearing clothes approximately 72,000 years ago.

🐾 The female pigeon cannot lay eggs if she is alone. In order for her ovaries to function, she must be able to see another pigeon. If no pigeon is available, her own reflection in a mirror will suffice.

🐾 Pigeons were used as messengers from the first century AD all the way through until the Second World War.

🐾 A flock of pigeons when flying together are known as a kit.

🎵 Pigeons coo.

🐾 A young pigeon up until four weeks of age is known as a squab.

A FLOCK OF PIGEONS

🐾 The tumbler pigeon is able to turn backward somersaults when in flight.

🐾 It is against the law to feed pigeons in New York City.

🐾 Pigeons produce milk. In the bird kingdom this is unique to them and flamingoes.

🐾 The dodo was a close relative of the pigeon. Extinct less than 100 years after being discovered by the Dutch in 1598, it was not a prolific species. The female laid just one egg a year.

♫ Seagulls squawk.

🐾 A seagull can drink saltwater because it has special glands that filter out the salt.

🐾 A flock of seagulls is sometimes referred to as a squabble or a screech.

🐾 The Belcher gull, named after British explorer Sir Edward Belcher, is the most serious enemy of the guano-producing birds of Peru.

🐾 Herring gulls have exhibited tool-use behaviour.

A FLOCK OF SEAGULLS

🐾 Collective nouns used for sheep also include a down, a hurtle and a trip. When a flock is deliberately driven it is correctly known as a drove or drift.

🐾 Sheep's milk is used to produce Roquefort cheese.

🐾 Sheep were the first domesticated ruminant and possibly the first animal domesticated by humans about 11,000 years ago.

🐾 Sheep's wool was being used by the Egyptians and Babylonians as long as 6,000 years ago.

🐾 Domestication has changed sheep so much and made them so helpless that they could not survive in the wild. The exception to this is the feral Hawaiian, first introduced as a domesticated breed to the island in the 1790s.

🐾 Sheep feature heavily in recorded human history. The Bible has more references to sheep and lambs than any other animal.

🐾 In 1996 a Finnish Dorset sheep named Dolly became the first mammal to be cloned, and consequently became the world's most famous sheep.

A FLOCK OF

♫ Sheep bleat
and baa.

🐾 Sheep can recognize
individual human faces and
are believed to be able to
remember them for years.

SHEEP

🐾 Common swifts are unable to sit on branches, but occasionally they hang from them.

🐾 Swifts capture insects, bathe, drink and, on occasion, mate while in flight.

🐾 Swifts have short legs and rest by clinging vertically.

A FLOCK OF SWIFTS

🐾 Despite a similarity to the swallow, swifts are more closely related to the hummingbird. Similarities to the swallow are based on convergent evolution and a lifestyle based around catching insects while in flight.

🐾 Many species of swift use saliva to glue their nests to a surface. The nest of the 'edible-nest' swiftlet is made entirely of saliva and is the main ingredient in the Chinese delicacy commonly known as 'bird's nest soup'.

A FLOTILLA OF FRIGATEBIRDS

🐾 Frigatebirds are sometimes known as 'pirate birds' because they commonly snatch food from the beaks of other seabirds.

🐾 Frigatebirds do not swim, cannot walk well, and cannot take off from a flat surface. They often stay aloft for more than a week.

🐾 The frigatebird has the largest wingspan to body weight ratio of any bird.

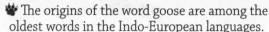 The origins of the word goose are among the oldest words in the Indo-European languages.

🐾 The first bird domesticated by humans was the goose.

🐾 While the eggs of the Canada goose are incubating, females lose their flight feathers and cannot fly until after their eggs hatch and the feathers regrow.

🐾 Strictly speaking the female is a goose while the male is a gander.

♫ Geese cackle, hiss and honk.

A GAGGLE OF GEESE

🐾 In medieval times it was believed that barnacle geese grew from barnacles. Catholics classified these geese as fish and therefore could eat them during Lent.

🐾 In the fifteenth century the noun 'gagyll' was used for both geese and women.

🐾 Domesticated geese have large fat deposits at their rear. This causes them to sit upright unlike their wild cousins and makes them unable to fly. Domesticated females lay up to 160 eggs a year compared to the 5–12 laid by wild geese.

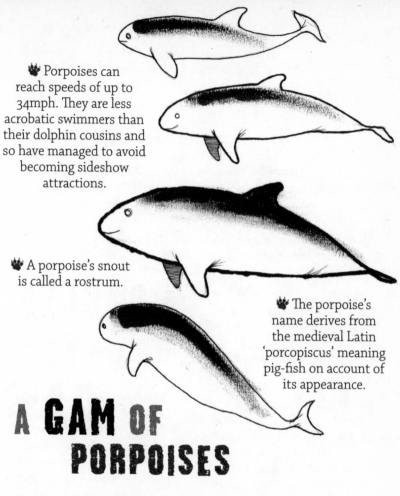

🐾 Porpoises can reach speeds of up to 34mph. They are less acrobatic swimmers than their dolphin cousins and so have managed to avoid becoming sideshow attractions.

🐾 A porpoise's snout is called a rostrum.

🐾 The porpoise's name derives from the medieval Latin 'porcopiscus' meaning pig-fish on account of its appearance.

A GAM OF PORPOISES

🐾 The term 'gam' originated from sailors on whaling trips encountering another ship out at sea. Voyages could last several years and crews would interact after being lifted to the other vessel by the use of the 'gamming chair'. Interestingly, 'porpoise' comes from 'pig fish' due to its appearance, and 'gammon' was the haunch of a swine which led to the eighteenth century slang word 'gams' referring to women's legs.

🐾 A group of whales is also known as a run or a herd. A small gam is called a pod of whales.

🐾 Whales are the closest living relative of the hippopotamus.

♫ Whales have their own language known to us as 'whale song'. They can create a range of sounds from simple clicks to haunting melodic song. They have been known to generate about 20,000 acoustic watts of sound at 163 decibels.

🐾 A blue whale's tongue weighs around 2.7 tons and its mouth is large enough to hold up to 90 tons of food and water.

🐾 A whale penis is called a dork.

🐾 The blue whale has a 5,000l lung capacity and can emit a 40ft vertical single column blow when breathing.

🐾 Like all mammals whales produce milk. A blue whale calf drinks approximately 400l per day. It weighs 3 tons at birth and reaches an average of 26 tons within twelve months.

A GAM

🐾 The blue whale is the largest known mammal that has ever lived and is the largest animal on the planet today. It can reach 105ft long and weigh 150 tons. The largest specimen recorded, caught in 1947, measured 90ft 6in and weighed in at 209 tons.

OF **WHALES**

❧ Whales are very long-lived creatures. In 2007
a huge bowhead whale killed by the Inuit in Alaska
was found to contain stone tools and part of a lance
manufactured and used in the 1880s, making
this whale at least 115 years old, while a recently
developed form of optical testing has shown one
bowhead whale to be over 200 years old.

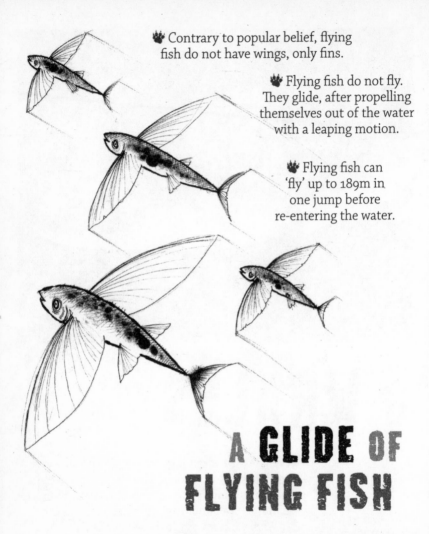

🐾 Contrary to popular belief, flying fish do not have wings, only fins.

🐾 Flying fish do not fly. They glide, after propelling themselves out of the water with a leaping motion.

🐾 Flying fish can 'fly' up to 189m in one jump before re-entering the water.

A GLIDE OF FLYING FISH

🐾 A carnivorous characin, related to the piranha, which is only found in the Amazon, actually does technically fly short distances by buzzing its wing-like fins.

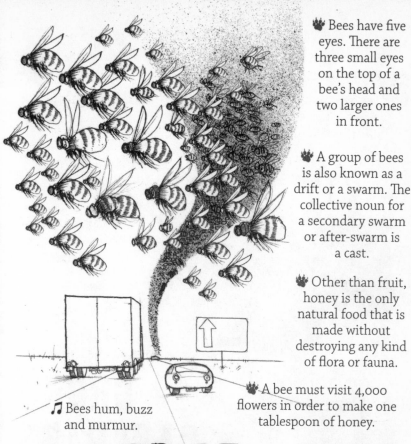

🐾 Bees have five eyes. There are three small eyes on the top of a bee's head and two larger ones in front.

🐾 A group of bees is also known as a drift or a swarm. The collective noun for a secondary swarm or after-swarm is a cast.

🐾 Other than fruit, honey is the only natural food that is made without destroying any kind of flora or fauna.

🐾 A bee must visit 4,000 flowers in order to make one tablespoon of honey.

♫ Bees hum, buzz and murmur.

A GRIST OF BEES

🐾 This phrase originates from the Old English word 'grist' which meant 'the action of grinding' – and the term 'grind' was first used with regard to wheat in about 1430. Nineteenth-century industrialization meant that one was less likely to keep one's nose to the grindstone and by 1828 grind meant any hard work and grist was used to refer to the hard-working bee.

🐾 The capybara of South America is the largest rodent in the world.

🐾 Capybara means 'master of the grasses' in the Guarani language.

🐾 The capybara is a herbivore and a fussy eater. 75 per cent of a capybara's diet comes from 3–6 species of plant.

🐾 Capybaras eat their own faeces as a source of bacteria.

♫ Capybaras purr and bark.

🐾 Capybaras can sleep underwater, keeping their noses just at the waterline.

A GROUP OF CAPYBARA

🐾 Their skin has the unusual characteristic of stretching in only one direction and as a result they are sought after for glove production.

🐾 Sixteenth-century missionaries mistook the capybara for an aquatic 'fish-like' animal. In some parts of South America local Catholics still claim a papal dispensation that allows the capybara to be eaten at Lent.

A GROUP OF GUINEA PIGS

♫ Guinea pigs squeak, cluck and whistle.

🐾 Guinea pigs live wild in areas of South America.

🐾 The predecessors of the Incas domesticated the guinea pig and farmed them for food.

🐾 Guinea pigs are still an important food source in Peru. They are so much a part of modern culture that Jesus and the disciples are shown dining on them in a portrait of the Last Supper housed in Cuzco's main cathedral.

🐾 Like humans, guinea pigs don't make their own vitamin C and so need to eat fresh vegetables.

🐾 Guinea pigs are very good swimmers.

🐾 The use of guinea pigs for scientific experimentation dates back at least to the seventeenth century and the term has become synonymous with scientific subjects of all species including humans.

🐾 When excited they often perform little hops in the air, known as 'popcorning' among guinea pig aficionados.

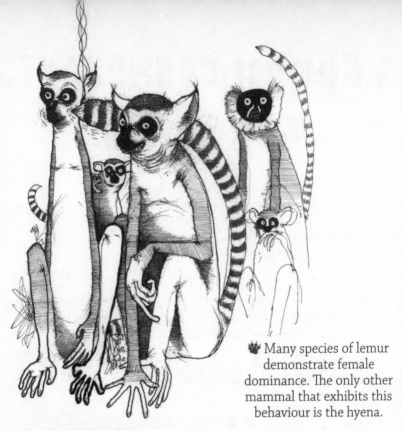

A GROUP OF LEMURS

🐾 Many species of lemur demonstrate female dominance. The only other mammal that exhibits this behaviour is the hyena.

🐾 Lemurs have nails rather than claws on all digits with the exception of the second toe of each hind foot. This digit is known as the 'toilet claw' and is used for grooming.

🐾 Ring-tailed lemurs enter into 'stink fights' over territories. They start by rubbing scent from their wrists onto their tails which are then waved at their rivals so that the scent can waft over. The battle is won by whoever produces the most potent odour.

A GULP OF CORMORANTS

🐾 The pelagic cormorant uses its own guano to glue its nest materials together and then to cement its nest to the cliff face.

🐾 Some Japanese rural communities use tame cormorants to catch fish. The cormorants are tethered by a leg to stop them flying off and are prevented from swallowing the fish they catch by a soft noose tied loosely around their throat.

A GULP OF SWALLOWS

🐾 When building their mud nest, swallows make up to 1,000 trips collecting mud.

🐾 Tree swallows 'fight' over feathers in mid-air in what is believed to be a form of play.

🐾 Swallows hunt insects while on the wing and forage at speeds of up to 40km per hour.

♫ Swallows titter.

All truly wild horses in the world today are actually feral horses and descended from domesticated horses. There is a small population of wild horses in Mongolia known as Przewalski's horse which had been extinct in the wild but was reintroduced in the late 1990s after a successful captive breeding programme.

Humans first began to domesticate horses in about 4500 BC. Horses have been used for transport, food, warfare, sport and entertainment as well as currency. Their importance has resulted in an extensive vocabulary used to describe equine-related matters from anatomy to size, colours, behaviour and locomotion.

A HARAS OF HORSES

♫ Horses neigh and whinny.

The underside of a horse's hoof is called a frog. The frog peels off several times a year with new growth.

Horses, zebras and donkeys can interbreed, but the offspring are usually sterile.

When a female horse and male donkey mate, the offspring is called a mule, but when a male horse and female donkey mate, the offspring is called a hinny.

Young horses are called foals with male ones known as colts and female ones as fillies. The collective noun for colts is a rag. The collective noun for mares is a stud.

🐾 A group of domestic horses is called a stable when the property of humans. The collective noun for both ponies and racehorses is a string.

🐾 All racehorses celebrate their birthday on 1 January.

🐾 The horse has the largest eye of any land mammal.

A HAREM OF SEALS

🐾 A small harem is known as a pod of seals.

🐾 Seals are also collectively known as a herd or a rookery.

🐾 The rare Hawaiian monk seal has been known to dive to about 1,650ft.

🐾 Elephant seals can hold their breath for up to two hours while diving.

🐾 One way to tell seals and sea lions apart is that sea lions have external ears and testicles.

🐾 Performing seals as found in circuses are actually sea lions.

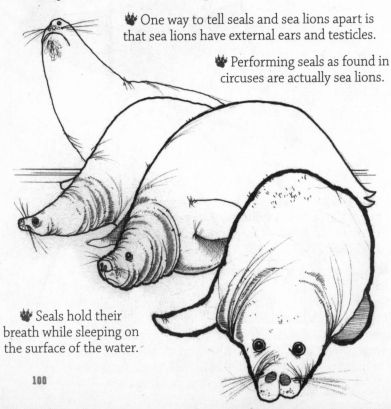

🐾 Seals hold their breath while sleeping on the surface of the water.

🐾 The flea has the highest peak blood pressure of any animal. Just before jumping, its blood reaches a pressure of 10 atmospheres.

A HATCH OF FLEAS

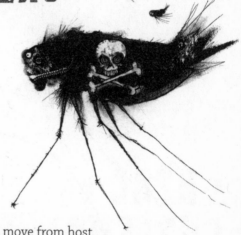

🐾 Female fleas consume fifteen times their weight daily.

🐾 Adult fleas can live for up to two years during which time the female can lay up to 1,200 eggs.

🐾 Fleas are wingless and move from host to host by jumping. Adults can survive away from a host for several weeks without eating.

🐾 Fleas have changed the course of human history more than any other animal. They have been the main carrier of plague which has killed immeasurable millions since the first recorded pandemic which began along the Mediterranean coast in AD 542. As carriers of the bubonic plague, fleas were responsible for killing up to one third of the population of Europe in the fourteenth century, with the majority of the blame falling on the flea-carrying rats.

A **HERD** OF **ASSES**

🐾 Wild asses live in herds of up to 1,000 animals.

🎵 Asses hee-haw and neigh.

🐾 A group of asses when driven in a group is correctly known as a drove unless they are in a roped line, in which case they are known as a coffle.

🐾 The donkey is descended from the African Nubian ass and is the oldest domestic beast of burden. It had been domesticated in Egypt by 4000 BC.

🐾 Although the bristle-thighed curlew was first described during Captain Cook's visits to Tahiti in the eighteenth century their summer nesting grounds weren't identified until 1948.

A **HERD** OF **CURLEWS**

🐾 The Eurasian curlew is the largest wading bird found in Europe. Their name is derived from the distinctive 'curl-oo' call they make.

🐾 The Far Eastern curlew, often just known as the curlew, is the largest migratory wading bird in the world.

🐾 Studying migratory patterns has led to the conclusion that Eskimo curlews were the most likely shorebirds to have attracted the attention of Christopher Columbus to the Americas on his first voyage. Once among the most plentiful American shorebirds, numbering in the tens of millions, they are now critically endangered, and possibly even extinct.

A HERD OF CATTLE

🐾 A herd of cattle is sometimes referred to as a mob.

🎵 Calves bleat and bulls bellow.

🐾 Today's cattle are descended from two species: wild aurochs, fierce and agile herd animals that populated Asia, North Africa and Europe, and Eotragus, an antelope-like, Asian forest creature.

🐾 The earliest evidence for the domestication of cattle is from Çatal Hüyük, a Neolithic settlement in Turkey that flourished *c*. 6500 to *c*. 5800 BC. At this time some species of sheep and goats were still being hunted.

🐾 In referring to domestic cattle a grown male is a bull, a grown female is a cow and an infant is a calf. A female that has not given birth is a heifer and a castrated male is a steer.

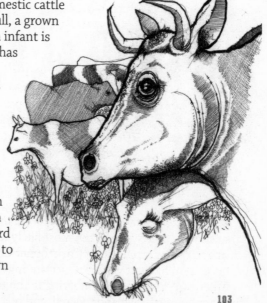

🐾 In various societies throughout human history wealth has been measured in terms of cattle. The word 'cattle' is closely related to 'chattel' and the modern word 'capital'.

A HERD of OXEN

🐾 The collective term for oxen in a harness is a team unless it is a pair in which case it is a yoke of oxen.

♫ Oxen low and bellow.

🐾 A bullock is a mature castrated male, also known as an ox. They are castrated to make them more docile and to put weight on more quickly than their non-castrated brethren. The collective noun for bullocks is a drove.

🐾 A traditional team of oxen consisted of eight animals that would follow the teamster's calls, with 'gee' traditionally used for a turn to the right and 'haw' for a turn to the left.

A HERD OF PIGS

🐾 A pig is a hog but a hog is not a pig. Hog is a generic name for all swine but in the terminology of swine breeding, a pig is a baby hog less than ten weeks old. The collective noun for hogs is a drove.

🎵 Pigs grunt, squeal and squeak.

🐾 A pig's squeal can reach up to 115 decibels, 3 decibels higher than the sound of a supersonic Concorde.

🐾 Some remote tribes in New Guinea treat pigs as symbols of wealth. It is not uncommon for women in these tribes to breastfeed orphaned pigs. Despite the close bond, these pigs are eventually eaten.

🐾 Pigs use mud as a sunscreen as they are susceptible to sunburn.

A HERD OF WRENS

🐾 The cactus wren builds many nests as decoys but actually lives in just one of them.

🐾 House wrens are fiercely territorial and have been known to destroy other birds' eggs by piercing them and removing them from the nest.

🐾 The male rock wren can have a large song repertoire of 100 or more song types. It learns many of these from its neighbours.

A HILL OF RUFFS

🐾 Ruffs are highly gregarious birds, with a wintering hill of almost a million birds reported in Senegal.

🐾 During the mating season the male ruff has collar-like erectile feathers around the neck and takes its name from the pleated circular collar in fashion in the sixteenth century.

🐾 The female ruff does not sport a ruff.

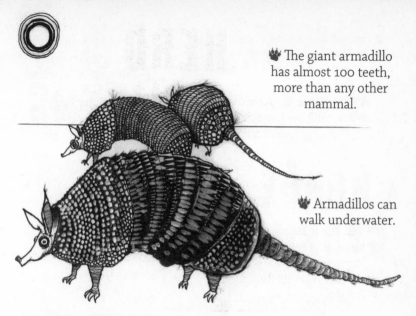

🐾 The giant armadillo has almost 100 teeth, more than any other mammal.

🐾 Armadillos can walk underwater.

🐾 The collective noun for the armadillo is believed to have originated during the Great Depression in America where they were often eaten instead of the 'chicken in every pot' that had been promised by President Herbert Hoover.

🐾 The armadillo's largest ancestor, the heavily armoured Glyptodon, was 16ft long and had a 10ft carapace on its back. It lived well into historical times and its body armour was used by some South American Indians for shelter.

🐾 Armadillos have four babies at a time and they are always all the same sex.

A HOOVER OF ARMADILLOS

🐾 Gerbils as pets are a recent addition. The Mongolian gerbil was first introduced as a pet in 1964.

🐾 Most pet gerbils in the world are descended from twenty pairs caught near the Amour river in Mongolia and Manchuria in 1935.

🐾 Lettuce is harmful to the gerbil as the nitrates it contains can prevent oxygenation of the blood.

🐾 Gerbils can survive without drinking water if they have plenty of moist food.

A HORDE OF GERBILS

🎵 Gerbils squeak. The purring sound that gerbils make is known as bruxing.

🐾 Between 20 per cent and 50 per cent of all pet gerbils have epilepsy. Seizures can be brought on by fright, stress or even a new environment.

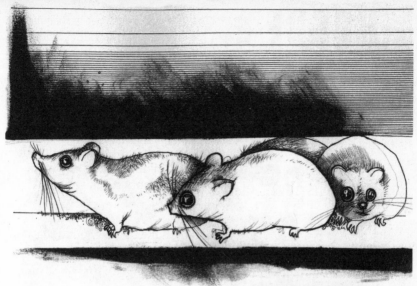

A HORDE OF HAMSTERS

🐾 Syrian hamsters are largely solitary in the wild and will normally fight to the death if put together.

🐾 In Australia it is illegal to keep hamsters as pets. It is thought that any hamsters that escape could breed and become pests.

🐾 Other than the golden hamster which is largely used as a domestic pet, most species of hamster are wild and nocturnal.

🐾 All pet hamsters are descended from a single female wild golden hamster found with a litter of twelve young in Syria in 1930.

🐾 Hamsters are excellent diggers; they create burrows with separate rooms for sleeping, food storage and excretion.

A HORDE OF INSECTS

♫ Beetles drone.

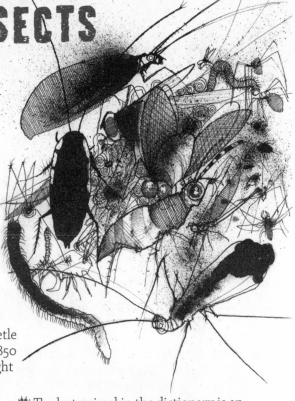

🐾 One in four animals on our planet is a beetle.

🐾 Each year insects eat up to one third of the Earth's food crop.

🐾 The practice of eating insects is called entomophagy.

🐾 A rhinoceros beetle can support up to 850 times its own weight on its back.

🐾 The last animal in the dictionary is an insect. The zyzzyva is a tropical weevil.

🐾 The name ladybird comes from the Middle Ages when they were known as the 'Beetle of Our Lady', named after the Virgin Mary who was often shown in religious paintings wearing a red cloak. The ladybird's bright colours are a warning to predators of its foul taste. As a further warning, when disturbed, the ladybird will secrete small amounts of its foul-smelling yellow blood from its legs.

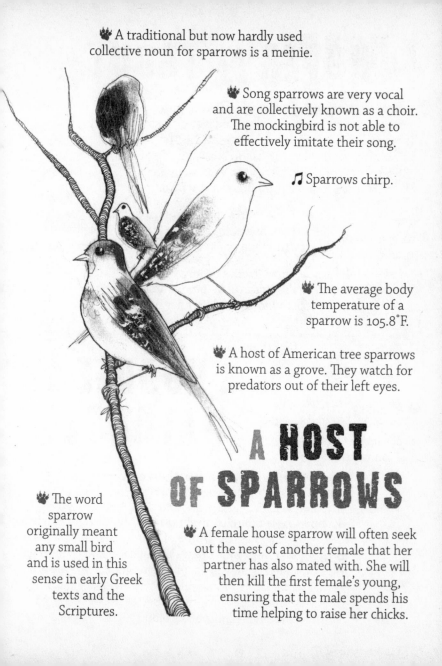

🐾 A traditional but now hardly used collective noun for sparrows is a meinie.

🐾 Song sparrows are very vocal and are collectively known as a choir. The mockingbird is not able to effectively imitate their song.

🎵 Sparrows chirp.

🐾 The average body temperature of a sparrow is 105.8°F.

🐾 A host of American tree sparrows is known as a grove. They watch for predators out of their left eyes.

A HOST OF SPARROWS

🐾 The word sparrow originally meant any small bird and is used in this sense in early Greek texts and the Scriptures.

🐾 A female house sparrow will often seek out the nest of another female that her partner has also mated with. She will then kill the first female's young, ensuring that the male spends his time helping to raise her chicks.

A HOVER OF TROUT

🐾 Fish farming and the artificial propagation
of fish was first practised by the ancient Chinese.
They collected fish eggs by placing mats in streams
or ponds and allowing the fish to spawn on them.
These mats containing fertilized eggs were then
sold for use in ponds and flooded rice fields.

🐾 In the fourteenth century, a French monk, Dom
Pinchon, discovered how to artificially fertilize trout
eggs and then hatch them by burying them in sand.

🐾 Female brown trout fake orgasms to
encourage males to ejaculate prematurely so
as to be able to move on to another mate.

A HUDDLE OF WALRUSES

🐾 The walrus, like pigs
and light-coloured horses,
can be sunburned.

🎵 Walruses roar. They make noise both above
and below the water. Above the water they
snort, click, roar, whistle, bark, grunt and rasp.
Below the water they click and tap.

🐾 Touch is an important sense in walrus communities and
they seek physical contact with each other when possible.

🐾 Walrus tusks can
reach 3ft in length.

🐾 A husk of hares is sometimes known as a drove, down, mute or trace.

🐾 The antelope jackrabbit, a type of hare, has been known to leap as high as 5ft and as far as 22ft.

🎵 Hares squeak.

🐾 Young hares are known as leverets.

🐾 Unlike rabbits, hares are born with hair and able to see.

🐾 Hares have not been domesticated.

A HUSK OF HARES

AN IMPLAUSIBILITY OF GNUS

🐾 The animal is also known as a wildebeest – an Afrikaans word meaning 'wild beast'.

🐾 The calves can stand and run within three to seven minutes of being born.

🎵 Wildebeests are also called gnus because their call sounds like 'gnu gnu'. Bulls have an array of loud vocalizations from moans to explosive snorts.

🐾 Wildebeests live in more densely packed herds than any other large mammal, except for humans.

🐾 Gnus and zebra graze in harmony because each animal prefers a different part of the same grass.

🐾 The current spectacle of wildebeest migration is a natural phenomenon that only started in the 1960s when the population grew from 250,000 to over 1.5 million. It is estimated that around 250,000 wildebeest die while on the annual migration circuit.

🐾 The largest species of cockroach live in South America and grow to 6in in length with a wingspan of 1ft.

🐾 Cockroaches are able to survive in very difficult conditions including on limited 'food' resources such as the glue from the back of postage stamps.

AN INTRUSION OF COCKROACHES

🐾 Cockroaches break wind every fifteen minutes and they even continue to release gas for up to eighteen hours after they die.

🐾 The dust created by cockroach droppings, dead specimens and cast-off cockroach skin is one of the causes of asthma.

🐾 In Brazil there's a species of cockroach that eats human eyelashes among its diet, usually those of young children while they are asleep, as they are attracted to the minerals and moisture from the tear ducts.

🐾 Cockroaches can survive a month without food and a week without water. A cockroach can even live a week without its head – it only eventually dies of thirst because without a mouth it can't drink.

A KINE OF COWS

🐾 The collective noun for a group of twelve cows is a flink.

🎵 Cows moo and low.

🐾 The Sanskrit word for 'war' means 'desire for more cows'.

🐾 The Maasai tribe of East Africa traditionally believes that all cows on Earth are the God-given property of the Maasai.

🐾 The greenhouse gas effect of methane produced by cows is twenty-three times greater than that of carbon dioxide. Scientists are looking at ways to reduce the levels of methane that cows produce, possibly by transferring to them a gas-reducing bacteria found in kangaroos.

A KNOB OF TOADS

🐾 As toads are considered part of the frog family they are often collectively known as a knot.

🐾 Contrary to popular belief, toads do not cause warts. And unlike a frog, a toad cannot jump.

🐾 The cane toad is the most widespread Latin American amphibian. It has very venomous skin and when attacked it oozes this poison into the predator's mouth. The venom contains a complex cocktail of fourteen chemicals which act on the heart and nervous system causing salivation, cardiac arrhythmia, high blood pressure, convulsions and ultimately death.

🐾 The cane toad was introduced to Australia to protect sugar-cane from beetle pests. In June 1935, 101 toads arrived at Edmonton, North Queensland with breeding beginning immediately. Within six months of being released, their offspring numbered over 60,000 young toads.

🐾 All frogs alive today are believed to be descended from the Stephens Island frog which lived about 150 million years ago and still lives today. Unusually, this frog does not have webbed toes.

🐾 The northern leopard frog uses its eyes to help it swallow prey such as a small cricket. It closes its eyes and retracts its eyeball into its body which pushes into the prey and helps force the food to the back of the oesophagus.

🎵 Frogs croak. People often describe a frog's croak as a 'ribbit'.

🐾 The collective noun for tadpoles is a cloud.

🐾 The poison-arrow frog has enough poison to kill about 2,200 people.

🐾 The Australian rocket frog is able to jump fifty times its body length.

A **KNOT** OF **FROGS**

🐾 The wood frog has a unique physiology that prevents damaging ice crystals forming within its cells. It is able to freeze solid during the winter and thaws out as the temperature rises in spring.

A LABOUR OF MOLES

🐾 A mole can dig 60ft of tunnel or more per day. This is equivalent to a man burrowing the length of two soccer pitches.

🐾 Naked mole rats are the only hairless mammals.

🐾 The golden mole is one of the strongest animals by size and body weight. A captive animal was able to exert a force equal to 150 times its own weight.

🐾 Mole saliva contains a toxin that paralyses earthworms so moles are able to store their still-living prey in underground larders. Studies have shown mole larders with up to 1,000 earthworms in them.

🐾 Up until the mid seventeenth century the mole was also known in Britain as the mouldywarp.

🐾 The star-nosed mole can locate, catch and eat food in under 300 milliseconds – faster than the human eye can detect.

🐾 A group of swans in the air is known as a wedge.

🐾 All the swans in England are the property of the monarch.

🐾 A group of swans on the ground is known as a bank.

🐾 A female swan is known as a pen while a male is known as a cob.

A LAMENTATION OF SWANS

♫ Swans crey and hiss.

🐾 A baby swan takes twenty-four hours to peck its way out of the shell and is known as a cygnet.

🐾 A swan is one of the very few birds with a penis. Most birds have no external sex organs and mate by joining their cloacae in a 'cloacal kiss'.

121

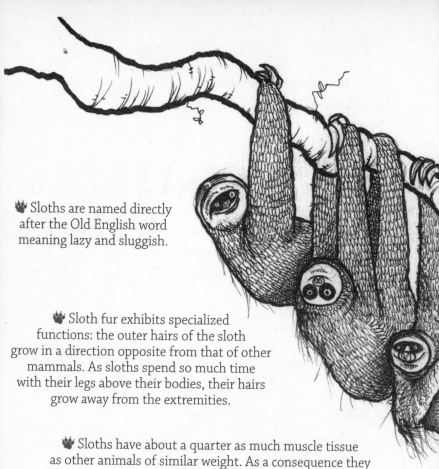

🐾 Sloths are named directly after the Old English word meaning lazy and sluggish.

🐾 Sloth fur exhibits specialized functions: the outer hairs of the sloth grow in a direction opposite from that of other mammals. As sloths spend so much time with their legs above their bodies, their hairs grow away from the extremities.

🐾 Sloths have about a quarter as much muscle tissue as other animals of similar weight. As a consequence they move only when necessary and even then very slowly.

A LAZINESS

🐾 Sloths have very sharp, strong claws. Sloths eat, sleep, and even give birth hanging upside down by their limbs from tree branches. They even sometimes remain hanging from branches after death which has proved a successful deterrent to human hunters.

🐾 It takes a sloth two weeks to digest the food it eats.

🐾 Sloths come down from the branches and go to ground about once a week to urinate and defecate. This is when they are at their most vulnerable as on the ground their maximum speed is 1.2mph.

🐾 The three-toed sloth is the world's slowest mammal. Its average ground speed is about 0.07mph with a maximum speed of 0.17mph when in the trees.

OF SLOTHS

🐾 A black panther is really a black leopard. There is no single cat called the panther. The name is commonly applied to the leopard, but it is also used to refer to the puma and the jaguar.

A LEAP OF LEOPARDS

🐾 Leopards can leap up to 18ft horizontally and up to 9ft vertically.

🎵 Leopards roar. The leopard's roar is a rough rasp said to sound like a handsaw cutting wood. However, neither the snow leopards of the high mountains in Central Asia nor the clouded leopards of Borneo can roar.

🐾 Although fiercely territorial, leopards retain their strong maternal bonds and mature females often have reunions with their mothers.

🐾 The leopard is a truly opportunistic hunter and consumes virtually any animal it can hunt down and catch. This ranges from dung beetles, rodents, birds and primates to antelope and deer.

🐾 Despite being predators of man's hominid ancestors, leopards do not normally attack humans unless they are unable to hunt for food. The infamous leopard known as 'Panar' killed and ate over 400 people after being injured by a poacher and thus being made unable to hunt normal prey. Panar was eventually killed by legendary hunter and conservationist Jim Corbett.

A **LEAP** of **LIZARDS**

🐾 The basilisks are lizards that are able to run on the surface of water. They are sometimes referred to as the 'Jesus Christ lizards'.

🐾 The tuatara lizard of New Zealand has three eyes – two in the centre of its head and one on top. Its metabolism is so slow that it only has to breathe once an hour.

🐾 Slow-worms look like snakes but are actually legless lizards. If you think you see one, remember that unlike snakes, lizards have eyelids and external ears.

🐾 Komodo dragons can reach 9ft in length. They have been known to stalk, attack and kill humans.

🐾 Many lizard species can undergo tail autonomy. They can lose the tail to distract or escape from a predator – it will grow back slimmer and shorter.

🐾 Although 'leap' is the correct term, 'lounge', as in lounge lizard, has started to appear as a common variation. While there is no historical basis for this term, the mass appeal of the internet will likely result in this becoming the recognized collective noun in the near future.

🐾 In Old English, a deer (or 'der') referred to many wild animals including fish, ants and foxes and it was only by the early sixteenth century that it lost its general meaning and was used to describe the deer as we know it. Prior to this a deer was known as a 'heorot'.

🐾 The given name 'Oscar' is derived from the Gaelic word meaning 'deer lover'.

A LEASH OF DEER

🐾 A male deer is often known as a buck. In the eighteenth century, the word 'buck' was used to describe a deerskin, which was used as a currency by the Native American Indians and the European settlers. In 1748 a cask of whisky was valued at 5 bucks. The buck was later replaced by the dollar.

🎵 Deer bell. Stags bellow and call.

🐾 Reindeer milk has more fat than cows' milk.

🐾 Deer in the wild tend to avoid humans. Despite this there are more than 1.5 million reported collisions between deer and vehicles every year in the US alone.

The only species of deer in which the females grow antlers is the reindeer.

The stem of the antler is called the beam, and the branches are known as tines.

A newborn Chinese water deer is so small that it can be held in the palm of the hand.

129

🐾 Although now mainly used for sport, greyhounds were used as hunting dogs by the Egyptians as long ago as 4000 BC and are able to bring down a small deer.

A LEASH OF GREYHOUNDS

🐾 The greyhound is the only dog mentioned by name in the King James Bible.

🐾 The greyhound has the largest heart of any breed of dog.

🐾 Greyhound racing originated from coursing. The first attempt at greyhound racing took place in the UK in 1876. Racing as we know it today first occurred in the US in 1912 with the invention of the mechanical lure.

🐾 The greyhound is the fastest breed of dog and can reach speeds of 45mph.

🐾 The dog in *The Simpsons*, Santa's Little Helper, is a greyhound.

🐾 The roadrunner is a large ground-dwelling cuckoo.

🐾 The roadrunner can reach speeds of 15mph.

A MARATHON OF ROADRUNNERS

🐾 As well as eating lizards and snakes, the roadrunner also eats small birds. When roadrunners catch their prey they pound them to death, then swallow the victim head first.

🎵 Roadrunners coo. The cartoon character Roadrunner who was constantly chased by Wile E. Coyote cried 'beep, beep!'

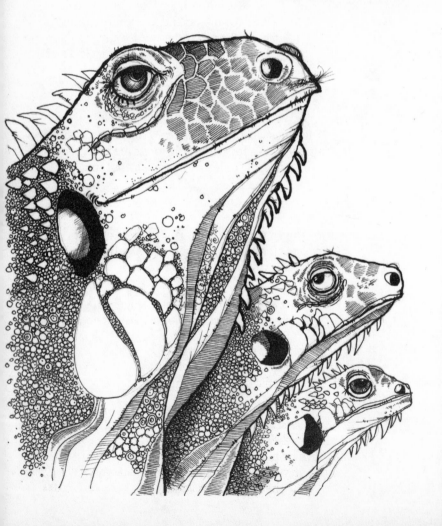

A MESS

OF IGUANAS

🐾 Common iguanas are arboreal. Wild iguanas spend most of their time on trees although some species have adapted to living in deserts and other difficult terrain.

🐾 Iguanas are able to hold their breath for up to thirty minutes.

🐾 Iguanas will often jump from tree to water and use their tails for swimming to escape predators. They are able to leap 40–50ft without injury.

🐾 Iguana meat is a valuable source of protein. In theory, farming iguanas could yield more meat per acre than cattle, while requiring only 70 per cent of what a chicken consumes. Fortunately for the iguana this is unlikely to happen.

🐾 The Galapagos marine iguana, the only sea-going lizard, is able to dive to a depth of 50ft.

🐾 The world's fastest reptile – measured on land – is the spiny-tailed iguana of Costa Rica which has been clocked at 21.7mph.

🐾 A previously unrecorded species of iguana was discovered in the Galapagos in 2009. Charles Darwin, who when he put forward his theory of evolution exactly 150 years earlier, had overlooked it when he visited the islands.

🎵 Hawks scream.

🐾 Other collective nouns for hawks are a cast, a kettle when flying or migrating in large numbers, and a boil when referring to a pair.

A MEWS OF HAWKS

🐾 Hawks have been scientifically shown to be of equal intelligence to the crow, considered the most intelligent of all birds.

🐾 The Cooper's hawk catches birds with its feet and uses its talons to crush birds. It is also not uncommon for it to drown its prey.

🐾 Adult sharp-shinned hawks pass food to their young in mid-air.

A MOB OF EMUS

🐾 The first verified occurrence of genetically identical avian twins was demonstrated in the emu.

🐾 Although extinct in Tasmania, the emu population on mainland Australia is higher today than it was prior to the arrival of Europeans.

🎵 The call of the emu consists of loud booming, grunting and drumming sounds that can be heard up to 2km away.

🐾 On very hot days emus pant to maintain their body temperature.

🐾 An Aboriginal myth is that the sun was created by throwing an emu egg into the sky.

🐾 Despite being avian, emu meat is considered to be red meat due to its colour and pH value.

♫ Sentry meerkats make a peeping sound when all is well. If they spot danger they bark loudly or whistle.

A MOB OF MEERKATS

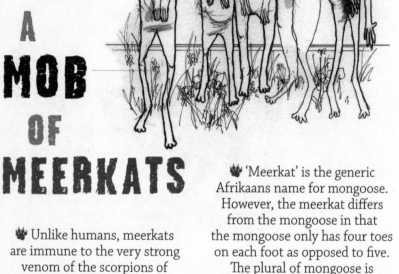

🐾 'Meerkat' is the generic Afrikaans name for mongoose. However, the meerkat differs from the mongoose in that the mongoose only has four toes on each foot as opposed to five. The plural of mongoose is mongooses and not mongeese.

🐾 Unlike humans, meerkats are immune to the very strong venom of the scorpions of the Kalahari desert.

🐾 Subordinate meerkat females will produce milk and suckle the dominant female's pups but have no pups of their own.

🐾 Meerkats were brought to Hawaii to kill rats. This plan failed because rats are nocturnal while the meerkat hunts during the day.

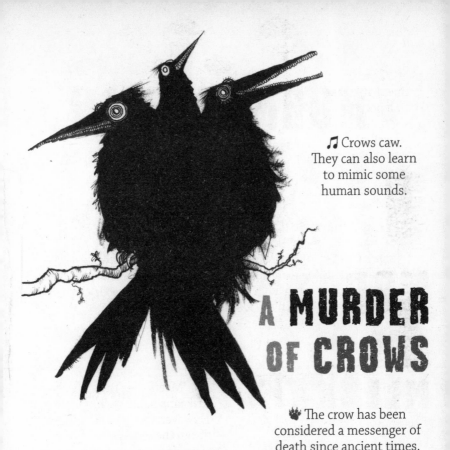

♫ Crows caw.
They can also learn
to mimic some
human sounds.

A MURDER
OF CROWS

🐾 The crow has been
considered a messenger of
death since ancient times.

🐾 Crows have the largest cerebral hemispheres,
relative to body size, of any avian family.

🐾 Crows are known to watch squirrels burying nuts
and then dig them up once the squirrel has gone.

🐾 Tool use by crows has been
documented and they are considered
the most intelligent of all birds.

A MURMURATION
OF STARLINGS

🐾 All of the more than 200 million European starlings found in North America today are descendants of approximately one hundred birds released in New York's Central Park in the early 1890s by an eccentric businessman who wanted to establish flocks in the US of all the species of birds referred to in the works of William Shakespeare.

🐾 Starlings compete aggressively for nesting sites. They may even evict the occupants of desired nest holes, including the woodpeckers that excavated them.

🐾 Starlings and their myna cousins are excellent mimics, able to copy the songs of up to twenty other bird species.

🐾 Starlings are drawn to the warm air over cities. Most notably, the tens of thousands of birds that fly in formation over Rome have resulted in numerous schemes to try to curb the shower of uric acid that falls from the skies during winter, damaging, cars, buildings and property.

A MUSTER OF PEACOCKS

🐾 The ornate display feathers of the peacock are known as a train.

🎵 Peacocks scream.

🐾 Peacocks have often been given great cultural significance. Considered immortal, the peacock was used as a symbol for the Catholic faith, and Lord Krishna's crown is always depicted containing a peacock's feather. Peacocks were considered to represent Mother Earth by the Dravidians of India and were worshipped as gods.

🐾 Although prized in the Middle Ages as a delicacy, it isn't a very tasty bird. Often the peacock was discarded and the plumage stuffed with the meat of a tastier bird such as a goose.

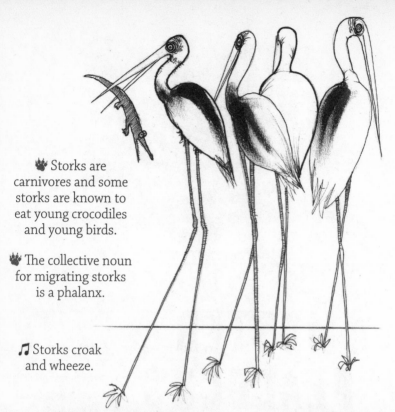

🐾 Storks are carnivores and some storks are known to eat young crocodiles and young birds.

🐾 The collective noun for migrating storks is a phalanx.

🎵 Storks croak and wheeze.

A MUSTERING OF STORKS

🐾 Storks fly with their necks extended, as opposed to herons which normally retract their necks. This being said, large storks like the marabou sometimes retract their necks to help support their heavy heads.

🐾 The wood stork hunts by touch alone, catching small fish the moment they touch its ultra-sensitive bill which can react within twenty-five milliseconds.

🐾 Wood storks have been known to fly as high as 6,000ft.

A MUTATION OF THRUSHES

🐾 The collective noun for the redwing,
a type of thrush, is a crowd.

🐾 The song thrush likes to eat snails. It
cracks the shells open by smashing them
against a stone with a flick of the head.

A NURSERY OF RACCOONS

🐾 The name 'raccoon' comes from the Algonquin
Indians word 'Arakun', which is translated as 'he
scratches with his hands'. This was recorded in 1607 by
Captain John Smith after his first meeting with Chief
Powhatan and his daughter Pocahontas.

🐾 The first written record of
the raccoon species was made
by Christopher Columbus.

🐾 The most important sense for
the raccoon is that of touch.

A NYE OF PHEASANTS

🐾 A group of pheasants in flight is known as a bouquet.

🐾 A pair of pheasants consisting of a male and female is called a brace. This term also applies to a pair of pheasants of any sex killed by hunting.

🐾 Male pheasants sometimes fight to the death for a harem of hens.

🐾 Bred primarily as a game bird, the pheasant is the most hunted bird in the world.

🐾 Pheasants were hunted by Stone Age humans but for food as opposed to the modern practice of hunting them as a sport.

🐾 Under the Game Act of 1831, open season for shooting pheasants in the UK is between 1 October and 1 February. Each year around 30 million are released – most survive less than a year.

🐾 The record for the number of downed pheasants is held by King George V of England who shot over 1,000 pheasants out of a total record bag of 3,937 over a six-day period in December 1913.

🐾 The first buffalo ever born in captivity was born at Chicago's Lincoln Park Zoo in 1884.

🐾 A group of buffalo is sometimes referred to as a herd or gang.

🐾 The term buffalo is used to describe animals in Africa and Asia and more commonly but mistakenly the North American bison.

🐾 The Great Plains of North America supported up to 30 million bison. By the end of the nineteenth century, and due to hunters like Buffalo Bill, fewer than 1,000 remained.

AN OBSTINACY OF BUFFALO

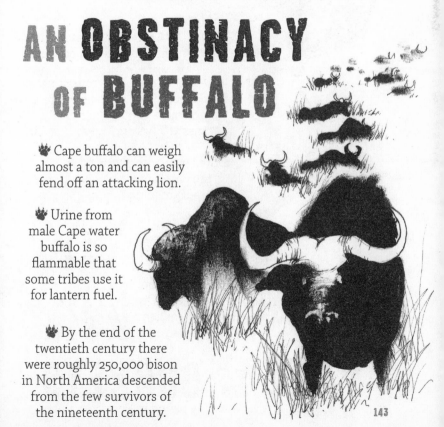

🐾 Cape buffalo can weigh almost a ton and can easily fend off an attacking lion.

🐾 Urine from male Cape water buffalo is so flammable that some tribes use it for lantern fuel.

🐾 By the end of the twentieth century there were roughly 250,000 bison in North America descended from the few survivors of the nineteenth century.

143

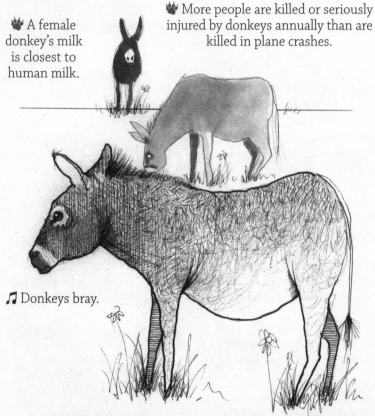

🐾 The placement of a donkey's eyes in its head enables it to see all four feet at all times.

🐾 Apparently a donkey will sink in quicksand but a mule won't and will have the strength to struggle out.

🐾 A female donkey's milk is closest to human milk.

🐾 More people are killed or seriously injured by donkeys annually than are killed in plane crashes.

♫ Donkeys bray.

A PACE OF DONKEYS

A PACK OF COYOTES

🐾 A pack of coyotes working together are able to take down a deer.

🎵 Coyotes yelp.

🐾 A hybrid between a dog and a coyote is called a coydog.

🐾 The coyote is considered a major threat to livestock in the US and over 20 million were killed during the twentieth century, including over 420,000 in 1988. Despite this, their numbers are increasing.

🐾 Other than humans, wolves are the natural enemy of the coyote. The superior learning ability of the coyote has created an unusual defence strategy. A coyote will often lead a pursuing wolf downhill, and then turn and run back uphill. The heavier wolf cannot stop in time and this gives the escaping coyote a huge lead.

🐾 Coyotes have extended their range throughout America to include urban and metropolitan areas. In 2006 a 35lb coyote, nicknamed Hal, was spotted in New York's Central Park. After a two-day chase he was finally caught on 79th Street.

🐾 Coyotes are one of the most persistent hunters in the animal kingdom. Successful attacks last from fourteen minutes up to almost twenty-one hours. Persistence is no guarantee of success; unsuccessful hunts lasting more than eight hours have been recorded before the coyotes gave up.

A PACK OF DOGS

🐾 A dog was killed by a meteor at Nakhla, Egypt, in 1911. The unfortunate and anonymous canine is the only creature known to have been killed by a meteor.

🎵 Dogs bark, woof and arf.

🐾 The pom-pom cut was originally developed to increase the poodle's swimming abilities as a retriever. The haircut allowed for faster swimming but the pom-poms were left to keep the joints warm.

🐾 All dogs are probably descended from an animal called Tomarctus which lived approximately 15 million years ago.

🐾 Mongrel dogs are known as curs. Their collective noun is a cowardice of curs.

🐾 At the end of the Beatles song 'A Day in the Life', an ultrasonic whistle, only audible to dogs, was recorded by Paul McCartney for his Shetland sheepdog.

🐾 Dogs are considered colour-blind and cannot see as well as humans. A dog sees objects first by their movement, second by their brightness, and third by their shape.

🐾 One of the first animals to be domesticated, dogs were not primarily used as food. Stone Age people tamed dogs to help them track game.

🐾 As a rule, cats and dogs get along better than cats and cats or dogs and dogs. So despite the phrase 'fighting like cats and dogs' being in common usage they are not natural enemies.

🐾 The term 'pack' was used to refer to a 'set of persons' in the thirteenth century and was only used as the collective noun for a group of hunting animals from the early fifteenth century.

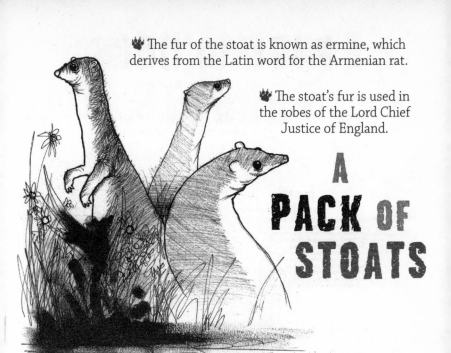

🐾 The fur of the stoat is known as ermine, which derives from the Latin word for the Armenian rat.

🐾 The stoat's fur is used in the robes of the Lord Chief Justice of England.

A PACK OF STOATS

🐾 50,000 ermine pelts were sent from Canada to England for King George VI's coronation in 1937.

🐾 Stoats have an unusual hunting strategy. An individual will approach a group of rabbits or birds and then jump around in a playful manner while seeming to ignore the potential prey. The prey are attracted to this odd performance, mesmerized in the case of rabbits, and edge nearer to watch, at which point the stoat pounces.

🐾 A stoat normally kills prey by biting into the base of the skull. Even when fully satisfied, a stoat will often kill prey to store for a future meal. In this case it kills by a different method. The stoat breaks the neck of the animal so that it will spoil less quickly.

147

A PANDEMONIUM of PARROTS

🐾 Parrots cannot eat chocolate because it is poisonous to them.

🐾 In the wild, macaws and cockatoos can fly 500 miles per day in search of food!

🐾 Parrots are monogamous breeders.

🎵 Parrots talk.

🐾 Wild parrots do not mimic sounds. Captive birds can imitate the speech and calls of other creatures. African grey parrots are the best mimics.

🐾 Because large parrots can live so long (more than seventy-five years), and may outlive their owners, it is often necessary for owners to make provision for them in their wills.

🐾 A parade of elephants is also known as a herd or a crash of elephants.

🐾 The elephant is the only mammal that can't jump.

🐾 Despite the size of their ears, elephants have poor hearing.

🐾 An elephant can smell water from 3 miles away.

🐾 During the Second World War, the very first bomb dropped on Berlin by the Allies killed the only elephant in Berlin Zoo.

🐾 The closest relative to the elephant is the manatee. It is believed that elephant ancestors crawled back into the sea to become manatees.

A PARADE OF ELEPHANTS

🎵 Elephants trumpet. Sounds made by an adult elephant are referred to as grunts, purrs, bellows, whistles and trumpeting.

🐾 Female elephants have a gestation period of twenty-two months.

🐾 Apart from humans, the only land animal that cries is the elephant.

A **PARCEL** OF

🐾 Adult penguins do not eat while on land, subsisting on a layer of fat under the skin.

🐾 Penguins seem to have no special fear of humans and have approached groups of explorers without hesitation. This is probably on account of there being no land predators in Antarctica.

♫ Baby penguins bleat.

PENGUINS

🐾 All penguins are countershaded – that is, they have a white underside and a dark upper side. This is to camouflage them in the water (a predator looking up from below has difficulty distinguishing between a white penguin belly and the reflective water surface).

🐾 Dives of the large Emperor penguin have been recorded which reach a depth of 565m (1,870ft) and last up to twenty-two minutes.

🐾 Penguins live in groups known as a colony and in some species young penguins assemble in large groups called crèches.

🐾 The name 'penguin' was first reliably reported from Newfoundland in a letter of 1578 and is said usually to have been pronounced 'pin-wing' with reference to its curiously rudimentary wings.

🐾 A much bandied about 'fact' is that nearly 3 per cent of the ice in Antarctic glaciers is penguin urine. This assumes that penguin urine has remained frozen for thousands of years without deteriorating. On that basis surely the Antarctic would be many metres deep in dead penguins too?

🐾 A wildlife myth is that penguins topple over backwards as they look up when aircraft fly overhead. This story seems to have begun circulating since aeroplane and helicopter pilots returned from the 1982 Falklands War. A team of scientists from the British Antarctic Survey were sent out to investigate and a five-week study of 1,000 King penguins showed that they did not fall over but did 'wobble a bit'.

🐾 An owl's feathers are so soft that they make no noise when in flight.

A PARLIAMENT
OF OWLS

🎵 Owls hoot, screech and wail.

🐾 The owl can catch a mouse in utter darkness, guided only by tiny sounds made by its prey.

🐾 Owls are far-sighted, and are unable to see anything clearly if within a few centimetres.

🐾 Owls are generally seen as harbingers of death or bad luck. In the West they are seen as a symbol of wisdom.

🐾 Ancient Egyptians used a representation of an owl for their hieroglyph for the sound 'm'.

A PARTY OF JAYS

🐾 Captive jays have been observed using tools such as strips of newspaper to rake in food pellets that have fallen outside their cages.

🐾 The word 'jay' was first recorded to describe the bird in 1310 and by 1623 had become a common English term to describe someone who was an 'impertinent chatterer' or a 'flashy dresser'.

A PASSEL OF OPOSSUMS

🐾 When opossums are 'playing possum' they have genuinely passed out from sheer terror. When threatened or harmed, they will mimic the appearance and smell of a sick or dead animal. Their bodies go stiff, their lips become drawn back with teeth bared, saliva foams around the mouth, and a foul-smelling fluid is secreted from the anal glands. After a period of time they regain consciousness.

🐾 Opossums are immune to the venom of many species of viper.

🐾 Opossums were used in one of the first 'tourist brochures' to promote the American colonies, 'A True Declaration of the Estate of the Colonie in Virginia' was published in 1610 with the reference: 'Apossouns, in shape like to pigges'. The word 'opossum' and its shortened form 'possum' were first recorded in 1613.

🐾 The mountain pygmy possum was first described in 1896 from fossil remains found at high altitude and was believed to be extinct. However in the 1960s, living specimens were found and the species was 'back' from extinction.

🐾 In Mexico the tails of the opossum are eaten as a folk remedy to improve fertility.

🐾 A group of hens is known as a brood.

🐾 Alektorophobia is the fear of chickens.

A PEEP OF CHICKENS

🎵 Chickens peep and cackle. Cocks crow.

🐾 The average laying hen lays 257 eggs a year.

🐾 A chicken with red ear lobes will produce brown eggs, and a chicken with white ear lobes will produce white eggs.

🐾 A bunch of eggs is known as a clutch.

🐾 A capon is a castrated cockerel. They are collectively known as a mews.

A baby platypus remains blind after birth for eleven weeks.

Female platypuses lack nipples. The young lick milk from the fur around the many small abdominal openings of the mammary glands.

The platypus and echidna are the most primitive living species of mammals.

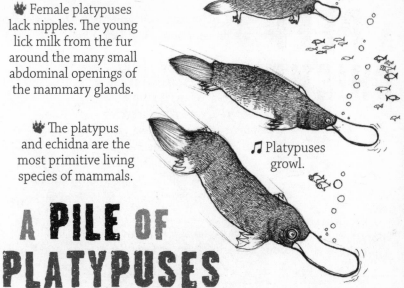

♫ Platypuses growl.

A PILE OF PLATYPUSES

The platypus was originally believed to be a hoax consisting of a mammal's body to which a duck's bill had been sown. Even after it was accepted as a true animal in 1800 it was only confirmed that it laid eggs in 1884. It is still known as the duck-billed platypus.

The platypus is one of the few mammals that are venomous. Males have a spur on the hind foot that delivers a venom capable of causing severe pain to humans.

Platypuses aren't the only egg-laying mammals on Earth. Echidnas, also known as spiny anteaters, also lay eggs. The platypus and the five known species of echidna make up the monotreme group of animals.

🐾 Young locusts are called nymphs.
A group of nymphs is known as a band.

🐾 A plague of locusts is often referred to as a swarm.
Presumably not to panic people living in its path.

🐾 When locust migration occurs, the locust
plagues are so dense that they blacken the sky over
an area of many miles. A plague may be 1,500m
high and has been known to cover hundreds of
square miles. The plagues can travel thousands of
miles and contain billions of insects.

🐾 A large plague of locusts can
eat 80,000 tons of corn in a day.

🐾 In 2004 a plague of locusts in Morocco was
recorded as 230km long, at least 150m wide, and
contained an estimated 69 billion locusts.

🐾 While most insects are considered to be
forbidden by kosher dietary laws, four varieties
of locust are listed in the Torah as permissible.

A PLAGUE OF LOCUSTS

🐾 A pod of dolphins is often referred to as a school which is the common collective for fish – the dolphin, of course, is a mammal.

🐾 Dolphins have an eye on each side of their head. Each eye moves independently of the other, so dolphins can see ahead, to the side, and behind them.

🐾 Dolphins probably have the best hearing of any animal. They receive sounds through their jawbone and head which create vibrations that pass into the tiny bones of their inner ear.

🎵 Dolphins click. As well as clicking they also use whistles to communicate with other dolphins. Every dolphin has a unique whistle which they use to identify each other.

🐾 Dolphins constantly shed their skin. Therefore, they have very few, if any, barnacles or parasites on them.

🐾 A dolphin's ultrasound ability is so sophisticated that it can detect a shark half a mile away and be able to tell if its stomach is full or empty.

🐾 60–65 million years ago dolphins and humans shared a common ancestor – the Mesonycid.

A POD OF DOLPHINS

🐾 The collective
noun for bottlenose
dolphins is a grind.

🐾 Dolphins have
belly buttons.

The quills of the African porcupine can be as long as 14in.

A PRICKLE OF PORCUPINES

A large porcupine can have over 30,000 quills covering its body.

Porcupine quills are loosely attached and a porcupine running into an enemy will leave them full of quills.

Porcupines are very fond of salt and will gnaw on wooden handles of tools just to taste the salty perspiration of humans.

🐾 The muzzle of a lion is like a fingerprint – no two lions have the same pattern of whiskers.

♫ Lions roar.

🐾 Lions cannot roar until they reach the age of two.

🐾 The name 'Singh' used by over 20 million Sikhs comes from an Ancient Indian Vedic name meaning 'lion'.

A PRIDE of LIONS

🐾 During the reign of Kublai Khan, the Chinese used lions on hunting expeditions. They trained the big cats to pursue and drag down animals such as wild bulls and to stay with the kill until the hunters arrived.

🐾 Depictions of lions have been dated back over 30,000 years. Lions featured as prominent symbols of cultures including the Babylonians, Hindus, Egyptians and the Kingdom of Judah. The lion remains the symbol of the city of Jerusalem.

🐾 The term 'pride' was first used in relation to a group of lions in 1486 but lions were not commonly seen en masse. A pride of lions only actually entered common usage in the 1930s.

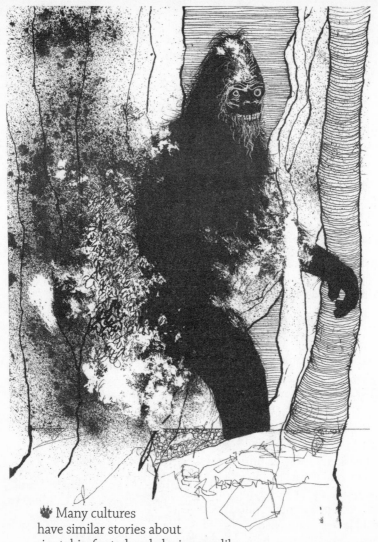

🐾 Many cultures
have similar stories about
giant, big-footed and elusive ape-like
humans, such as the Yeren of China, the Orang Pendek
of Sumatra, the Yeti of the Himalayas, the Yowie of
Australia and the Mapinguari of South America.

The word 'sasquatch' means 'hairy man' in the Halkomelem language of British Columbia. Sasquatch or Big Foot has been sighted since the 1800s all across the Pacific Northwest. Their collective noun comes from the strong odour that witnesses have smelled.

Sasquatch is omnivorous, nocturnal and reportedly a good swimmer.

Sasquatch is said to be between 9ft and 15ft in height. Footprints have reached 2ft in length although 75 per cent of recorded footprints have been proven to be faked.

A PUNGENT OF SASQUATCH

In my view the most likely theory is that sasquatch are Neanderthals who survived extinction due to their remote habitat and the lack of interaction with modern man. This is not as unlikely as it at first sounds. Remains of the previously unknown *Homo floresiensis* were found recently in Indonesia which showed that the species survived on the island of Flores until at least as recently as 12,000 years ago, making it the longest-lasting non-modern human discovered so far, surviving long past the Neanderthals which became extinct about 24,000 years ago. Locals, who would have no knowledge of the fossil remains, claimed the existence of small, hairy cave dwellers called Ebu Gogo which were still present during the sixteenth century and were reported up until the late nineteenth century. The fossils were only excavated in the twentieth century.

A QUANTITY OF SMELT

🐾 The candlefish is so oily at spawning time that it can be dried and burned as a candle.

🐾 Smelt roe is bright orange in colour, and is often used to garnish sushi.

A RABBLE OF BUTTERFLIES

🐾 Some species need sodium and get it from a variety of sources, from dung to licking the sweat off humans.

🐾 Butterflies get their name from the yellow brimstone butterfly that is first seen in the early spring or 'butter' season.

🐾 The monarch butterfly migrates from Mexico to North America, a journey of over 2,500 miles.

🐾 Butterflies taste with their hind feet.

🐾 Sea otters swim on their backs and eat in this position.

🐾 Sea otters have 200,000 strands of hair per cm of skin.

A RAFT OF SEA OTTERS

🐾 Sea otters need to eat up to 25 per cent of their body weight every day in order to survive.

🐾 Unlike most marine mammals, sea otters do not have a layer of insulating blubber but rely on air trapped in their fur for warmth. They often top up this layer of air by blowing into their fur.

🐾 The collective noun for a group of male turkeys is a posse although rafter is still commonly used.

🐾 Native Americans rarely ate turkey. To them, killing such a timid bird was thought to indicate laziness.

A RAFTER OF TURKEYS

🐾 Most domestic turkeys today are bred for food and their breasts are so large that they must rely on artificial insemination as they can't get close enough to mate.

🐾 *Sesame Street*'s Big Bird allegedly wears over 4,000 turkey feathers dyed yellow.

🐾 Astronauts Neil Armstrong and Edwin 'Buzz' Aldrin ate turkey in foil packets for their first meal on the moon.

🐾 Wild turkeys can fly at speeds of up to 55mph over short distances and can glide as far as a mile without flapping their wings.

🐾 In Turkey what is almost universally known throughout the rest of the world as the 'turkey' is known as the 'large bird' or 'Hindi' while in Hebrew the word is the same for both the bird and country of India. The Indian link is a result of confusion between the discovery of the New World and the original assumption that this was in fact a new route to India.

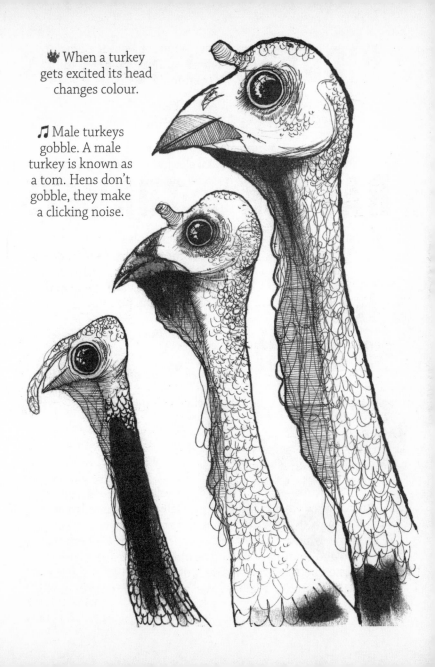

🦃 When a turkey gets excited its head changes colour.

🎵 Male turkeys gobble. A male turkey is known as a tom. Hens don't gobble, they make a clicking noise.

A RICHNESS OF MARTENS

🐾 The more traditional but less used collective noun for the marten is a richesse.

🐾 For commercial purposes, the pelt of the marten, an animal closely related to the skunk and the weasel, is known in the US as American sable.

🐾 A snail can sleep for three years.

🐾 Sometimes the word escargatoire is used as the collective noun for snails. However, this actually refers to a group of snails in a man-made snail farm. Heliciculture is the farming of snails.

A ROUT OF SNAILS

🐾 A snail only mates once.

🐾 Only twelve of the approximately 74,000 species of snail are used as food by humans.

🐾 Most land snails move by gliding along on their muscular foot, which is lubricated with mucus. This mucus allows them to slide over sharp objects like razors without injury.

🐾 Snails were eaten by early humans and were considered a delicacy by the Romans. Unlike most Roman 'delicacies' snails are still considered a speciality food today.

A **ROUT** OF WOLVES

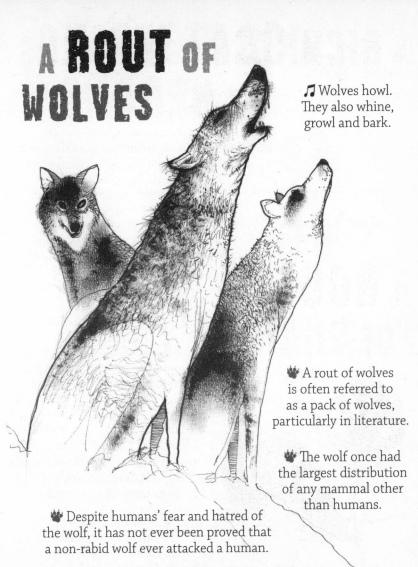

♫ Wolves howl. They also whine, growl and bark.

🐾 A rout of wolves is often referred to as a pack of wolves, particularly in literature.

🐾 The wolf once had the largest distribution of any mammal other than humans.

🐾 Despite humans' fear and hatred of the wolf, it has not ever been proved that a non-rabid wolf ever attacked a human.

🐾 A running wolf can clear 16ft in a single bound.

A SCATTERING
OF HERONS

🐾 Herons are sometimes collectively referred to as a seige or sedge. Interestingly, 'seige' does not follow the 'i' before 'e' rule and so I believe that this is a misspelling of the more obvious 'siege'.

🐾 A very large group of roosting or nesting herons is known as a heronry.

🐾 Herons stamp and peck at mosquitoes around their feet up to 3,000 times an hour. This prevents more then 80 per cent of the mosquitoes from feeding on the heron's blood.

🐾 Green herons are one of the few birds to use tools when hunting. They will drop bait including mayflies and feathers and then strike at the fish that come to investigate.

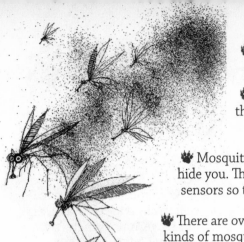

🐾 Mosquitoes dislike citronella because it irritates their feet.

🐾 Mosquitoes are attracted to the colour blue twice as much as to any other colour.

🐾 Mosquito repellents don't repel. They hide you. The spray blocks the mosquito's sensors so they don't know you're there.

🐾 There are over 3,000 different kinds of mosquito in the world.

🐾 A mosquito wing beats from 300 to 600 times per second. A male mosquito can find females by listening to the sound of their wings beating. It identifies the correct species by the pitch of the female's wings.

🐾 It is estimated that the mosquito has been directly or indirectly responsible for the death of 50 per cent of all humans who have ever lived. Even in the twenty-first century they kill up to one person every twelve seconds (probably the same time it has taken you to read this fact).

🐾 Mosquitoes are the most dangerous animals in the world. According to the World Health Organization there are 300–500 million clinical cases of malaria each year, resulting in 1.5–2.7 million deaths. Only female mosquitoes bite. Male mosquitoes feed only on nectar from plants.

A SCOURGE OF MOSQUITOES

A SEDGE OF BITTERNS

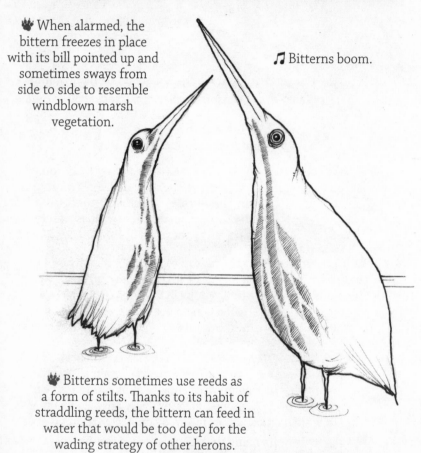

When alarmed, the bittern freezes in place with its bill pointed up and sometimes sways from side to side to resemble windblown marsh vegetation.

♫ Bitterns boom.

Bitterns sometimes use reeds as a form of stilts. Thanks to its habit of straddling reeds, the bittern can feed in water that would be too deep for the wading strategy of other herons.

Bitterns hide by standing upright with their bill pointed upward. This, coupled with their camouflage pattern, sees them imitating the reeds and tall grasses of their habitat.

🐾 A baby eel is called an elver.

🐾 Eel blood is toxic.

🐾 Electric eels can reach up to 2m in length and larger specimens can generate 500V of electricity. Despite its name the electric eel is in fact not an eel but is closely related to the carp.

A SEETHING OF EELS

🐾 A common myth is that sharks are the only animals that never get sick and are immune to every known disease including cancer. Sadly this has been proved not to be true.

🐾 On a beach holiday, you are more likely to die from a coconut falling on your head than a shark attack.

A SHIVER OF SHARKS

🐾 The teeth of the shark are embedded in the flesh and not in the jaw and are constantly replaced as they are lost. A shark can go through as many as 30,000 teeth in its lifetime.

🐾 The whale shark is the worlds largest fish. The largest specimen ever caught was captured in 1949 and measured 41ft 6in with an estimated weight of between 15 and 21 tons.

🐾 The largest eggs in the world are laid by a shark.

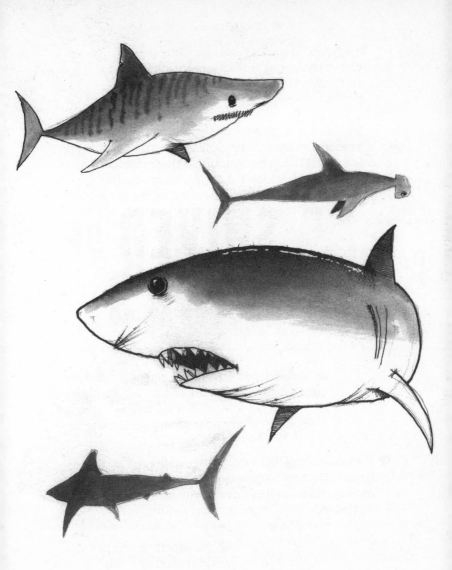

🐾 A shoal of fish in motion is known as a run.

🐾 The plural of fish in one species is fish. The plural of fish which contain several different breeds is fishes.

🐾 A shoal is a group of fish (or fishes) which has come together deliberately. If the group of fish is tightly organized and moves at the same speed in the same direction then it is known as a school such as a school of anchovies. Fish that just happen to be in the same place, normally for feeding purposes, are collectively known as an aggregation.

A SHOAL OF FISH

🐾 Other commonly used collective nouns for fish are a catch (when caught) and a draught (when specifically caught with a net).

🐾 Species of fish range in length from about 10mm to up to 20m in the case of the whale shark.

🐾 Members of different species tolerate temperatures ranging from freezing to over 100°F.

🐾 Up until the sixteenth century animals including crocodiles, seals and whales were classified as fish by natural historians.

🐾 Ketchup was originally a fish sauce first recorded in the Malay language in 1711 as 'kichap' and originating from the Chinese 'koechiap' meaning 'brine of fish'. It arrived in the US in fish form and was known as 'catsup' and it finally caught on when sailors started adding tomatoes to it.

A SHOAL OF OCTOPUSES

🐾 The correct plural for the octopus is octopuses although octopi is also in common use. The plural term for dead octopuses is actually octopus.

🐾 The Pacific giant octopus, the largest octopus in the world, grows from the size of a pea up to as much as 30ft across its arm span in only two years, its entire lifespan.

🐾 The male blanket octopus is 40,000 times smaller than the female. His mating technique involves tearing off his mating arm, placing it somewhere on the female's body and then swimming off to die.

🐾 Octopuses have three hearts.

🐾 The main colouring agent of octopus ink is melanin – the same chemical that gives humans their hair and skin colour.

🐾 Despite being only a few inches across, the venomous blue-ringed octopus has enough poison to kill a human.

A SHREWDNESS OF APES

🐾 Although this collective noun is normally used for all apes, it excludes the gorilla which was 'discovered' later and has its own collective term.

🐾 Apes differ from other primates (excluding humans) in that they do not have a tail and they do have an appendix.

🐾 Gibbons are unusual in that they are monogamous and have elongated legs which make them efficient bipeds.

🐾 Chimpanzees are the closest living relative to humans. We share 98.4 per cent of our DNA with them although some scientists estimate this could be as much as 99.4 per cent.

♫ Apes gibber.

🐾 Chimpanzees use medicinal plants to treat themselves for illness and injury. They also use tools when performing various actions.

🐾 Chimpanzees who share a territory move about in groups of varying sizes known as parties while the collective term for all the individuals in one territory is a community – just like their human cousins.

🐾 The sandhill crane is the oldest species of bird still alive today. A crane fossil structurally identical to the modern sandhill crane has been found in the US and has been dated as being approximately 10 million years old.

🐾 The main cause of death for adult whooping cranes in the US is collisions with power lines during migration.

A SIEGE of CRANES

🐾 A group of cranes is also known as a sedge or a herd.

🐾 It was commonly believed that cranes had transformed into birds from women. Julius Caesar noted in the first century BC that the ancient Britons refused to eat the flesh of the crane as they feared it had been human in a previous life.

🐾 Cranes have been symbolic and cultural references since ancient times. The longest ongoing tradition is the crane dance which has been performed in the courtyard of the Tongdosa Temple, South Korea, since the seventh century AD.

🐾 According to Japanese tradition, if you fold 1,000 origami cranes good health will be granted.

🐾 The word pedigree comes from the Old French phrase, 'pie de grue', which means 'foot of a crane' as the lines on a family tree were seen as a similar pattern.

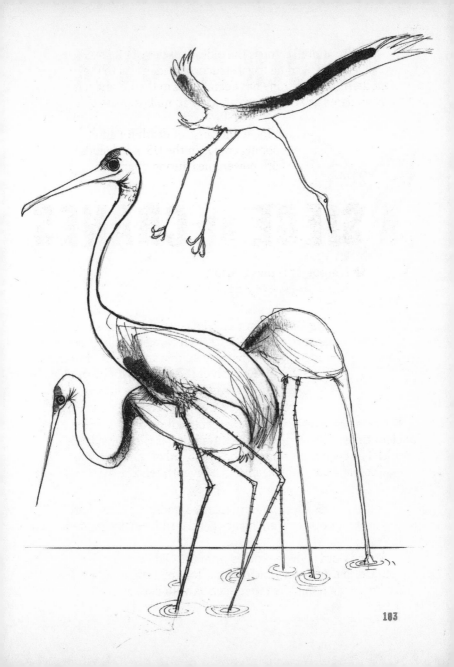

A SKULK OF FOXES

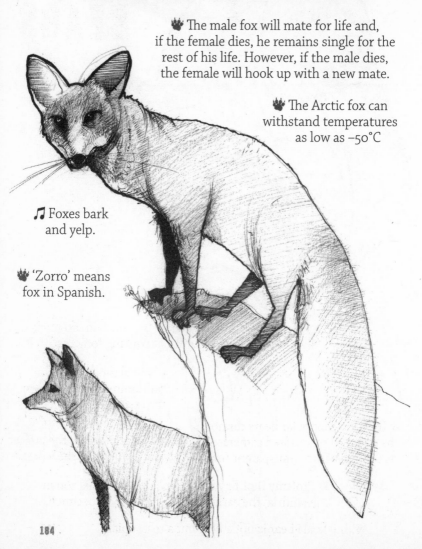

The male fox will mate for life and, if the female dies, he remains single for the rest of his life. However, if the male dies, the female will hook up with a new mate.

The Arctic fox can withstand temperatures as low as −50°C

♫ Foxes bark and yelp.

'Zorro' means fox in Spanish.

A SLOTH OF BEARS

♫ Bears growl.

🐾 Polar bears can swim 60 miles without pausing for a rest.

🐾 Polar bears are the only animals with hair on the soles of their feet.

🐾 It is said that polar bears cannot be detected by infrared cameras, due to their thick transparent fur.

🐾 The grizzly bear is the largest land carnivore in the world.

🐾 Ptolemy II of Egypt had a polar bear in his zoo in Alexandria, the earliest recorded captive specimen.

🐾 The koala bear is not a bear but a marsupial.

185

🐾 Jellyfish have been around for more than 650 million years which means that they pre-date the dinosaurs and the sharks.

A SMACK OF JELLYFISH

🐾 The box jellyfish kills more people than any other marine animal. The venom in one box jellyfish could kill sixty people.

🐾 The tentacles of the Portuguese man-of-war can reach up to 100ft in length. Even detached tentacles are capable of causing stings to humans for up to two weeks.

🐾 Jellyfish have an incomplete digestive system and therefore use the same orifice for intake of food and expulsion of waste materials.

🐾 The largest jellyfish ever recorded was an Arctic giant found in 1870 whose bell had a diameter of 7ft 6in while its tentacles stretched to over 120ft.

🐾 Jellyfish don't have brains.

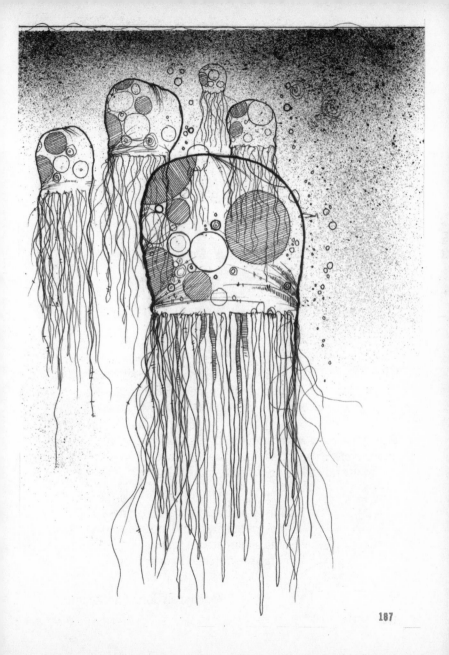

A SOUNDER OF WILD BOAR

🐾 Wild boar can and do breed with domestic and feral pigs.

🐾 Up until the 1930s toothbrushes were made from boar bristles.

🐾 Boar are very good swimmers.

🐾 Wild boar became extinct in Britain by the thirteenth century. Various attempts to reintroduce them over the centuries failed. However, the boar has reintroduced itself, with breeding sounders springing up at the end of the twentieth century from escapees from zoos and farms.

🐾 The collective noun for domesticated boar is a singular of boar. The collective noun for tame swine in general is a doylt while a general term for a group of wild swine is a herd.

A SPRING OF TEAL

🐾 Although considered a type of duck, recent molecular testing has proven that the teal is not related to any species of living duck.

🎵 Teal emit high-pitched 'peeps' and nasal quacks.

🐾 The female cinnamon teal creates a nest below dead vegetation so that it is hidden from all sides including from above. She enters the nest through a concealed side tunnel.

A STEAM OF MINNOWS

🐾 The largest species of the true minnow family is the carp.

🐾 Although minnows are a stand-alone species, the term 'minnow' is also used to represent the young of many species of fish.

🐾 A steam of minnows as a phrase refers to a general collection of tiny freshwater fish used as fishing bait.

🐾 Using bait for fishing has been practised since man first used tools. As other methods of hunting slipped away or were refined and industrialized, traditional fishing became a sport which has remained a major pastime (or an art and science depending on whom you talk to) since Izaak Walton wrote *The Compleat Angler; or, the Contemplative Man's Recreation* in 1653.

🐾 The major ingredient of skunk scent is (E)-2-butene-1-thiol, which the human nose can detect at a concentration of only 10 parts per billion. At very high concentrations this chemical is lethal.

A SURFEIT OF SKUNKS

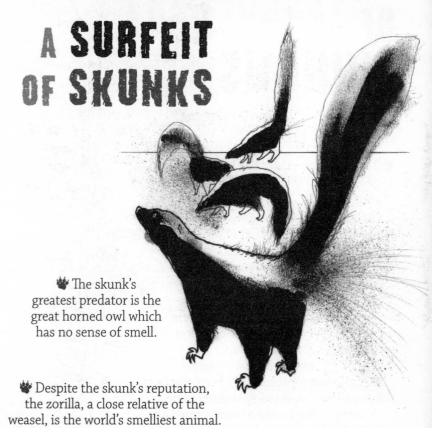

🐾 The skunk's greatest predator is the great horned owl which has no sense of smell.

🐾 Despite the skunk's reputation, the zorilla, a close relative of the weasel, is the world's smelliest animal.

🐾 Skunks cannot see more than 3m away and as a result more than 50 per cent of skunk deaths are the result of human activity, with roadkill being one of the most common causes of death. Fewer than 10 per cent of skunks live for more than three years.

A SWARM OF GRASSHOPPERS

♫ Grasshoppers chirp and pitter.

🐾 The term 'grasshopper' has traditionally been used for someone who has much to learn. References to this can be found from Aesop's fables in the sixth century BC to the television show *Kung Fu* in the 1970s.

🐾 Species of grasshopper that change colour and behaviour at high population densities are known as locusts.

🐾 Grasshoppers can jump forty times the length of their bodies.

🐾 Scandinavian lemmings are famous for moving in huge numbers over the countryside and jumping into the ocean in an apparent act of suicide. This is in fact not an act of suicide: the lemming just sees rivers, lakes, cliffs and even oceans as obstacles to cross in its search for food.

🐾 This migration, sometimes referred to as a 'death march', occurs periodically when the population explodes to the point that it outgrows local food sources.

A SWARM

🐾 Lemmings found in the Arctic regions of Asia and North America are pure white in winter and brown or reddish in summer. This seasonal colour change is unique among rodents.

🐾 Despite being able to swim they are not keen swimmers. Unfortunately, their instinct to find food outweighs their instinct for self-preservation and they can swim out to sea until unable to return.

OF LEMMINGS

Moths are found on all
land masses except Antarctica.

🐾 The venom produced by the caterpillar of the South American silk moth is powerful enough to cause a human to haemorrhage to death.

🐾 Clothing moths feed on clothing and natural fibres. They are able to turn keratin, a protein present in hair and wool, into food. They prefer dirty fabric and are particularly attracted to material containing human sweat.

🐾 The wings of the hummingbird hawk-moth beat so fast that they produce an audible hum.

🐾 The *Mabra elephantophila* moth drinks the tears of elephants as they contain salt, water and traces of protein.

A SWARM OF MOTHS

A TITTERING OF MAGPIES

♫ Magpies chatter.

🐾 Magpies have been known to kill old, sick or newborn sheep and cows by pecking them.

🐾 The European magpie is the only non-mammal known to be able to recognize itself in a mirror.

🐾 Unlike most birds, the black-billed magpie can use scent to locate food.

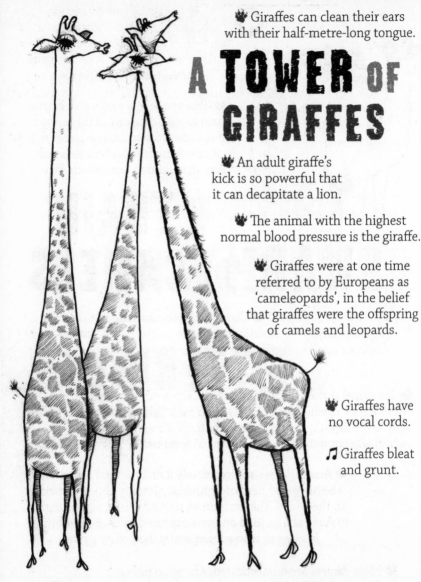

🐾 Giraffes can clean their ears with their half-metre-long tongue.

A TOWER OF GIRAFFES

🐾 An adult giraffe's kick is so powerful that it can decapitate a lion.

🐾 The animal with the highest normal blood pressure is the giraffe.

🐾 Giraffes were at one time referred to by Europeans as 'cameleopards', in the belief that giraffes were the offspring of camels and leopards.

🐾 Giraffes have no vocal cords.

🎵 Giraffes bleat and grunt.

A train of camels used as beasts of burden is known as a caravan of camels. A group of camels in the wild is a herd. A caravan and train travel in single file.

The camel first evolved in North America and died out in the ice ages, but some had emigrated across the ice bridges and survived in South America, Eurasia and North Africa.

A TRAIN OF CAMELS

Camel milk does not curdle.

Camel's-hair brushes are not made of camel's hair but from the long hairs from the tail of a squirrel, while camel yarn is actually spun from the hair of the Angora goat.

The camel is the only animal to have replaced the wheel in areas where the wheel had already been established. The camel only lost this unique role in the twentieth century when the wheel was combined with the internal combustion engine.

Australia has approximately a million feral camels and the only wild herd of dromedary (one-humped camels) in the world. The first camel, named Harry, was brought to Australia in 1840 and was executed in 1846 after biting his owner who subsequently died of gangrene.

Most camels are domesticated. About 90 per cent of the world's 14 million camels are dromedaries.

197

A TRIP OF GOATS

🐾 Goats were first domesticated by man 8,000–10,000 years ago and there are now over two 200 domesticated breeds.

🐾 Goats are used for meat, milk, and fibre including mohair, cashmere and angora.

🐾 Goat meat is eaten by more people worldwide than any other meat.

🐾 Goats are great swimmers.

🐾 A goat's pupils are rectangular.

🐾 Goats are considered to be of superior intelligence to dogs.

🐾 In Morocco goats climb argan trees to get to the berries.

🐾 Scientists have mixed a goat with a spider to create a goat that produces spider's silk in its milk. The normal-looking goats are in fact only 1/70,000 spider. By inserting just one spider gene into a goat's egg, the adult goat produces milk that can be processed to create an incredibly strong spider's silk fabric estimated to be five times as strong as steel.

🐾 It is believed that the original motivation for the domestication of the cat was to reduce mouse and rat populations.

🐾 The mortality rate of young mice is about 90 per cent.

♫ Mice squeak and squeal.

🐾 A female mouse can have up to eight litters per year with up to sixteen young per litter.

🐾 A male mouse is called a buck, a female mouse is called a doe and a baby mouse is called a pinky or a kitten.

🐾 The mouse was commonly used in folk medicine and was seen as a potential cure for bed-wetting. The medicinal mouse was either fried and roasted or reduced to a powder and mixed with water.

🐾 Some genetically engineered mice have hearts that glow green every time they beat.

A TRIP

🐾 Apparently Walt Disney was afraid of mice. Mickey Mouse was the first ever cartoon character to talk. In 1929's *The Karnival Kid*, Mickey's first words were 'Hot dogs'.

OF MICE

A TROGLE OF SNAKES

🐾 Other collective nouns used for snakes are a rhumba of rattlesnakes, a nest of vipers and a quiver of cobras.

🐾 A group of snakes is also known as a knot.

🐾 The Australian brown snake's venom is so powerful that only 1/14,000 oz is needed to kill a human being.

🐾 The poisonous copperhead snake smells like freshly cut cucumbers.

🐾 The anaconda, one of the world's largest snakes, gives birth to its young instead of laying eggs.

🐾 The viper's venom is harmless as long as it does not mingle with blood. Human experimenters have tasted and swallowed it, and fortunately afterwards were no worse off than before. Do not try this at home.

🐾 Snakes do not urinate. They secrete and excrete uric acid, which is a solid, chalky, usually white substance.

🐾 A troop of baboons is sometimes referred to as a congress.

🐾 The Ancient Egyptians worshipped a baboon god called Babi.

🎵 Baboons use over thirty vocalizations ranging from grunts to barks to screams.

🐾 Baboons have little fear of any animal including man. They are able to successfully take on leopards, which are their biggest predator.

🐾 During a fight with another baboon a male will often 'kidnap' an infant to use as a defensive hostage.

A TROOP OF BABOONS

🐾 Unlike other four-legged mammals, kangaroos cannot walk backwards.

A TROOP OF KANGAROOS

🐾 The grey kangaroo can jump more than 30ft in a single bound.

🐾 A newborn kangaroo is about 1in in length and can grow to 7ft tall.

🐾 Male kangaroos are called boomers, females are called flyers, and their young are called joeys.

The word kangaroo originates from 'gangurru' referring to a species of kangaroo in the Aboriginal language of Guugu Yimidhirr. Contrary to myth it does not mean 'I don't know' and the correct term was known to Captain James Cook.

Tree kangaroos found in the rainforests of New Guinea and northern Australia climb well and can leap from branch to branch.

The Kurnai aborigines used stuffed kangaroo scrotums as a ball for the traditional game of Marn Grook.

Kangaroos are unable to walk at slow speeds due to their large feet. Instead they push themselves forward, which involves using their shorter forelimbs and their tail as a tripod, in a movement known as crawl walking.

Kangaroos are good swimmers. If pursued into water, a large kangaroo may use its forepaws to hold the predator underwater so as to drown it.

🐾 Many species of dogfish are actually small sharks. The spiny dogfish is the most common shark in the Western Atlantic and dogfish species also include the distinctive leopard sharks.

🐾 Dogfish will latch onto almost anything put in the water including human hands.

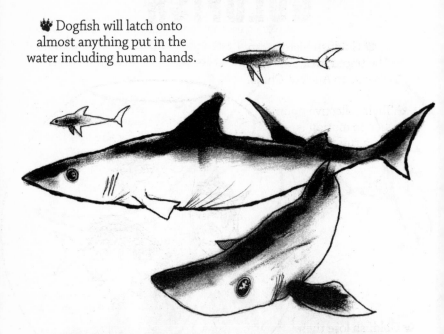

A TROOP OF DOGFISH

🐾 Dogfish have venomous spines at the base of their dorsal fins, which although not deadly to humans can take months to recover from if stung.

🐾 In Europe dogfish are sold as 'rock salmon' to make them sound more palatable.

A TROUBLING OF GOLDFISH

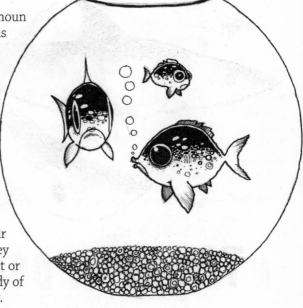

🐾 Goldfish history can be traced back over 1,500 years to Ancient China.

🐾 Their collective noun when in motion is a run.

🐾 Goldfish lose their golden colour if they are kept in dim light or are placed in a body of running water.

🐾 Contrary to popular belief, a pregnant goldfish is not called 'a twit'. Goldfish do not get pregnant. The female lays her eggs directly into the water and the male fertilizes them there. For goldfish aficionados the term 'twit' refers to a female as she is laying her eggs.

🐾 A tortoise is a terrestrial turtle

🎵 Turtles grunt.

A TURN OF TURTLES

🐾 The female green turtle sheds tears as she lays her eggs on the beach. This washes sand particles out of her eyes and rids her body of excess salt.

🐾 Turtles can read the magnetic map of their native area and imprint this into their memories. By reading variations in the Earth's magnetic fields the turtles are able to navigate across thousands of miles of ocean with pinpoint accuracy.

🐾 Researchers have recently discovered that, unlike most animals, a turtle's organs do not gradually break down as it ages or become less efficient over time.

🐾 The largest turtle ever recorded was a leatherback washed up on a beach in Wales in 1988. It measured over 9ft 5in from end to end and 9ft across its front flippers. This extraordinary specimen weighed in at 2,120lb.

🐾 Ravens are not fussy eaters. Items on the menu can include eggs and young of other birds, invertebrates, carrion, vertebrates, insects, refuse and rodents.

🐾 Charles II gave the first ravens to the Tower of London where it is believed that if they fly away the country and the crown will be destroyed. An older tradition is that the great King Arthur lived on as a raven.

🎵 Ravens croak.

🐾 Ravens are playful and have a wide range of actions that seem to be for amusement only. These range from pulling the tails of dogs to flying upside down.

🐾 Groups of ravens post sentries while they feed.

🐾 Ravens can imitate a number of sounds including the human voice.

AN UNKINDNESS OF RAVENS

🐾 The impressive aerial courtship display of the common buzzard is known as 'the rollercoaster'.

🐾 Augur buzzards are intensely territorial. Their territories are regularly used for thirty years or more.

🐾 The buzzard is the most abundant bird of prey in the UK. Feeding predominantly on rabbits, their numbers were dramatically reduced in the 1950s after myxomatosis killed off 99 per cent of their rabbit prey. In recent years their population has exploded, which is good news for them although bad news for rabbits.

🐾 Only a small part of the diet of the honey buzzard consists of mammals and reptiles. They mainly break open bee and wasp nests to feed on the insects and their larvae inside.

A WAKE OF BUZZARDS

A WALK OF SNIPE

🐾 The snipe's clutch size is almost always four eggs. When the first two chicks hatch, the male takes them away from the nest and cares for them separately while the remaining two chicks are cared for solely by the female. After they part the two groups do not interact.

🎵 The jack snipe has a sound likened to a galloping horse.

🐾 To attract a mate the male snipe produces a sound known as 'winnowing'. This is not created vocally but is produced by the flow of air over specially modified tail feathers.

🐾 Snipe are considered elusive birds that are difficult to hunt. This characteristic gave us the word 'sniper' first used by the British in India in the late eighteenth century to denote a hunter skilled enough to shoot this species of bird.

A WATCH OF NIGHTINGALES

🐾 The original form of the word 'nightingale' means 'night songstress' as early writers assumed that it was the female that sang. It is actually the male that sings.

🐾 In medieval times the collective noun for nightingales was an enchantment due to its beautiful song, but the term 'watch' gained prominence in the eighteenth and nineteenth centuries due to the popular fable of a nightingale that keeps guard.

🐾 Nightingales are so named because they frequently sing at night as well as during the day. The name has been used for over 1,000 years, 'nihtingale' being the form used by the Anglo-Saxons.

♫ Nightingales pipe, warble and jug-jug.

🐾 Gorillas were first spotted by the Carthaginian explorer Hanno before 480 BC. He thought they were a tribe of mainly hairy women and a few men, known by his interpreters as the 'Gorillae'. They were next recorded in 1847 and were known as the Pongo until renamed in honour of Hanno's discovery.

🐾 A whoop of gorillas is sometimes referred to as a band or troop.

🐾 They eat leaves, stalks and shoots. (I hope my grammar is correct.)

🐾 Humans are the gorilla's only enemy.

🐾 Gorillas have individual fingerprints.

🐾 Gorillas can catch human colds and other illnesses.

🐾 A gorilla named Koko has mastered up to 1,000 words in sign language. She describes herself as a 'fine animal person gorilla'.

A WHOOP OF GORILLAS

🐾 A young male gorilla is called a blackback. He's almost as big as a silverback, but his hair (not fur) has not as yet changed colour.

🐾 A wobble of ostriches is also commonly known as a troop.

🐾 An ostrich's eye is almost 2in (5cm) across, the largest eye of any land animal.

🐾 Ostriches stretch out their necks and lay their heads on the ground to keep from being seen – contrary to popular belief they do not bury their heads in the sand as they would suffocate.

🐾 The ostrich is the largest and heaviest living bird.

🐾 Ostriches can run at up to 70km an hour and can outpace most pursuers.

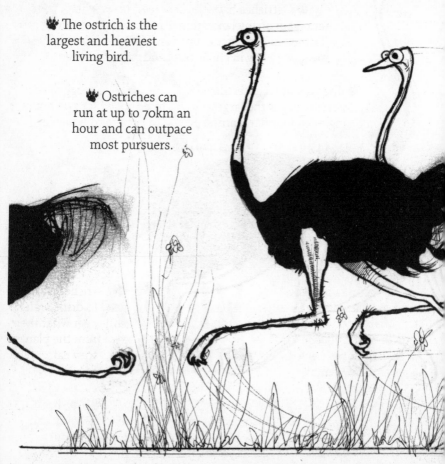

A WOBBLE OF OSTRICHES

🐾 Ostriches have the best feed-to-weight ratio gain of any land animal and are successfully farmed in over fifty countries. The meat is a red meat, very low in cholesterol and almost fat free.

🐾 The yolk in an unfertilized ostrich's egg is the largest single cell found in nature.

🐾 An ostrich egg needs to be boiled for two hours to get a hard-boiled egg.

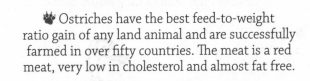

🐾 Ostriches do not need to drink water as they get what they need from the plants they eat.

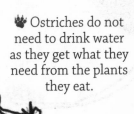

🐾 Flycatchers aggressively defend their nests and harass larger birds such as crows and hawks. The olive-sided flycatcher has been recorded knocking squirrels off trees.

🐾 Male Hammond's flycatchers defend their territory so violently during the mating season that they often get locked together in mid-air while in aerial 'combat'.

🐾 The male vermilion flycatcher, sometimes known as Darwin's flycatcher, often tries to win over a potential mate by bringing her a butterfly as a gift.

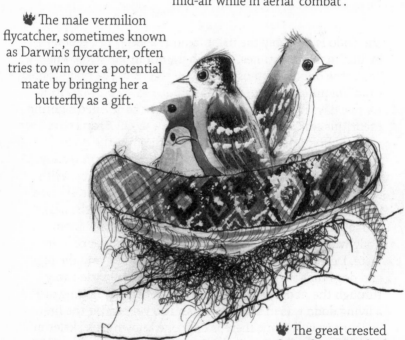

🐾 The great crested flycatcher uses shed snake skins as part of its nest lining. This is believed to ward off predators.

A ZAPPER OF FLYCATCHERS

AFTERWORD
DEAD AS A DODO

The dodo is arguably the most famous species to become
extinct in modern times. Amazingly, not much is known
about the dodo. The most extensive record of the dodo comes
from Volquard Iversen, who was shipwrecked on Mauritius
for five days in 1662 and provides the last confirmed sighting.
Mauritius was first sighted by Portuguese sailors in 1507
and was first inhabited in 1598 at which point the dodo
was first recorded. Dodos ate seeds and fruits, both readily
available on the forest floor in their native Mauritius. With
a plentiful food supply and no predators, dodos had evolved
into flightless birds. Dutch sailors who arrived on the island
in 1598 found them tough and inedible and named them
'walghvogel' meaning nauseating fowl with reference to its
taste. Despite this, thousands were slaughtered and the pigs
and dogs that the sailors brought with them ate their way
through the dodos' eggs. The last unconfirmed sighting of
a living dodo was in 1681, less than 100 years after the first
encounter with man. There is only one known true skeleton
of a dodo, which is on display in the American Museum of
Natural History. The remains of the last known stuffed dodo
were kept in Oxford's Ashmolean Museum, but by 1755 the
specimen had decayed and was discarded save for the head
and a foot. The dodo was 'discovered' and killed off so quickly

that there is no collective noun specific to dodos. As far as the dodo was concerned, that was the end of that.

Few took particular notice of the extinct bird. The dodo passed without much attention so that by the early nineteenth century its existence was believed by many to be a myth. Written reports about newly discovered dodo bones in 1865 coincided with the publication of Lewis Carroll's *Alice's Adventures in Wonderland* and catapulted the dodo into public consciousness. The dodo has now become an emblem to showcase the importance of preserving the species we share the planet with.

This was the first but not the last time in recorded history that humans had wiped out an entire species. We do not seem to have learned from our mistakes. Perhaps it is not too late.

One of the ingrained features of human DNA is the subconscious urge to learn. As a species we see it as part of our remit to pass knowledge between each other. Language is one of the key driving forces in this quest for knowledge which has resulted in every aspect of life on Earth and even beyond this planet – whether it be living creatures, inanimate objects, feelings, behavioural patterns, fiction, natural forces, the past, the future, chemical reactions, the supernatural, social conditions, hypothetical situations or the impossible – having a distinctive way of being referred to.

Collective nouns are just that. They are terms used to describe groups of animals. In order for this rich addition to language to remain relevant we need to ensure there are groups of animals for us to continue naming.

When I started compiling this book it became very clear that most of the species are in some danger of losing their habitat, their quality and way of life, or even their very existence. In nearly every case this is a direct result of the influence of man.

Despite the incredible divergence of species, all species including man share common ancestors. Studying human DNA has resulted in the calculation that about 200,000 years ago there lived an 'African Eve' who is believed to have been ancestral to all living humans. An interesting view of our common ancestors has been put forward by Richard Dawkins who in his 'Gaps In The Mind' asks us to imagine holding your mother by the left hand. She in turn is holding her mother by the left hand; her mother is holding her grandmother and so on. This chain of ancestors would stretch less than 300 miles before reaching the common ancestor we share with the chimpanzee. Next we are asked to imagine this common ancestor holding her daughter with her other hand. She in turn is holding hands with her daughter and so on. By the time the chain had made its way back you would be facing a modern-day chimpanzee which (or who) shares at least 98.4 per cent of its DNA with us and is truly an animal cousin.

I sincerely hope that all the creatures featured in *A Mess of Iguanas...* continue to exist alongside us. It would be great if an updated version of this book would not only accommodate the collective nouns from newly discovered species but also include all the species found here. I hope that with consideration for these wonderful creatures we can create a situation for them that fits the immortal words written by Stan Laurel (1880–1965) and spoken by Oliver Hardy (1892–1957):

'WELL, HERE'S ANOTHER NICE MESS YOU'VE GOTTEN ME INTO'

USEFUL SOURCES AND INTERESTING READING

Attenborough, David (1979), *Life on Earth: A Natural History*.

Attenborough, David (1990), *The Trials of Life*.

Barnes, Juliana (1486), *The Boke of St Albans*.

Bernes, Julyans (Juliana Barnes), *Treatyse on Fysshynge with an Angle* (also found in Wynkyn de Worde's publication of *The Boke of St Albans*).

Berry, Edward (2001), *Shakespeare and the Hunt: A Cultural and Social Study*.

Bryson, Bill (2003), *A Short History of Nearly Everything*.

Carwardine, Mark (2007), *Natural History Museum Animal Records*.

Corbett, Jim (1948), *The Man-eating Leopard of Rudraprayag*.

Darwin, Charles (1859), *On the Origin of Species by Means of Natural Selection, or, The Preservation of Favoured Races in the Struggle for Life*.

Darwin, Charles (1871), *The Descent of Man*.

Dawkins, Richard (2001), *River Out of Eden: A Darwinian View of Life*.

du Fouilloux, Jacques (1561), *La Vénerie*.

Eccles, W. J. (1983), *The Canadian Frontier, 1534–1760*.

Gascoigne, George (1575), *The Noble Art of Venery and Hunting*.

Markham, Gervase (1595), *The Gentleman's Academic*.

Narby, Jeremy (1999), *Cosmic Serpent: DNA and the Origins of Knowledge*.

Nielsen, Claus (1995), *Animal Evolution: Interrelationships of the Living Phyla*.

Oxford English Dictionary (2005).

Phoebus, Gaston (*c.* 1389 and illustrated in the early fifteenth century), *Book of the Hunt*.

Smith, John (1608), *Map of Virginia, with a Description of the Countrey, the Commodities, People, Government and Religion*.

Svensson, Lars, Peter J. Grant, Killian Mullarney and Dan Zetterstrom (1999), *Collins Bird Guide: The Most Complete Guide to the Birds of Britain and Europe*.

Wallechinsky, David and Amy Wallace (2005), *The Book Of Lists: The Original Compendium of Curious Information*.

Walton, Izaak (1653), *The Compleat Angler; or, the Contemplative Man's Recreation*.

Warwick, Hugh (2008), *A Prickly Affair – My Life With Hedgehogs*.

Winston, Robert (2004), *Human: The Definitive Guide to Our Species*.

Zoological Society of London (1830– ongoing), *The Journal of Zoology*.

Zoological Society of London (1864–1980), *Zoological Record*, transferred and continued by BIOSIS / Thomson Reuters (1980– ongoing).

ANIMALTASTIC PLACES TO VISIT

KILL NOTHING BUT TIME, TAKE NOTHING BUT PHOTOGRAPHS AND LEAVE NOTHING BUT FOOTPRINTS

- The Okavango Delta, Botswana
- Taronga Zoo, Sydney*
- Singapore Zoo*
- The Serengeti National Park, Tanzania
- London Zoo*
- San Diego Zoo and the San Diego Wild Animal Park*
- National Zoological Gardens, Pretoria*
- Jurong Bird Park, Singapore*
- The Ngorongoro Crater, Tanzania
- The Natural History Museum, London
- Borneo's Gunung Mulu and Kinabalu National Parks as well as the Sepilok Orangutan Sanctuary
- The Southern Pantanal, Brazil
- Galapagos Islands
- Gombe Stream National Park, Tanzania, www.janegoodall.org.uk

* Zoos listed here are leaders in conservation and pioneers in creating as natural and stimulating a habitat as possible for their 'guests'.

INDEX

A page number in **bold** refers to where a heading has a main section devoted to it.